THE BASICS

Buddhism: The Basics provides a thorough and accessible introduction to a fascinating religion. Examining the historical development of Buddhism and its presence today, this guide covers:

- principal traditions
- practices and beliefs
- ethical guidelines and philosophy
- religious texts
- community

With helpful features including a detailed map of the Buddhist world, glossary of terms, and tips for further study, this is an ideal text for students and interested readers wanting to familiarise themselves with the Buddhist faith.

Cathy Cantwell is an academic researcher at the Oriental Institute, University of Oxford. She specialises in Tibetan Buddhism, and has worked on eleventh-century manuscripts, an eighteenth-century scriptural collection, and contemporary Buddhist ritual manuals and practice. She has taught widely in UK Higher Education and is joint author of *Early Tibetan Documents on Phur pa from Dunhuang*.

The Basics

BUDDHISM

THE BASICS

cathy cantwell

LONDON AND NEW YORK

First published 2010
by Routledge
2 Park Square, Milton Park, Abingdon, Oxon, OX14 4RN

Simultaneously published in the USA and Canada
by Routledge
270 Madison Avenue, New York, NY 10016

Routledge is an imprint of the Taylor and Francis Group, an informa business

© 2010 Cathy Cantwell

Typeset in Bembo and ScalaSans by
Taylor & Francis Books
Printed and bound in Great Britain by
CPI Antony Rowe, Chippenham, Wiltshire

British Library Cataloguing in Publication Data
A catalogue record for this book is available from the British Library

Library of Congress Cataloging in Publication Data
Cantwell, Cathy.
Buddhism : the basics / Cathy Cantwell.
    p. cm. – (The basics)
  1. Buddhism. I. Title.
  BQ4012.C36 2009
  294.3–dc22

                                    2009002030

ISBN10: 0-415-40879-2 (hbk)
ISBN10: 0-415-40880-6 (pbk)
ISBN10: 0-203-87425-0 (ebk)

ISBN13: 978-0-415-40879-0 (hbk)
ISBN13: 978-0-415-40880-6 (pbk)
ISBN13: 978-0-203-87425-7 (ebk)

CONTENTS

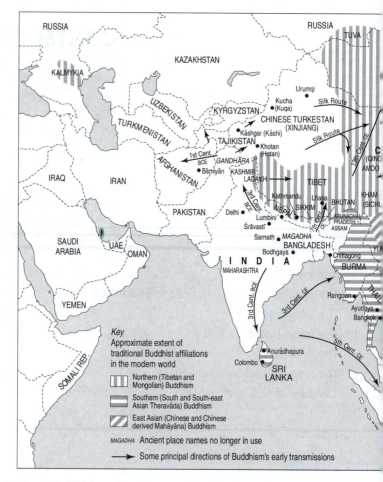

Map of Buddhism in Asia   Showing the main directions of the
historical spread of Buddhism, and the approximate locations of the major
Buddhist regions in the modern world

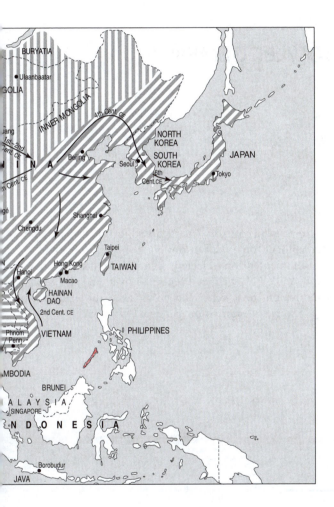

ACKNOWLEDGEMENTS

I would like to thank Professor Peter Harvey for his detailed and very helpful comments on a draft of this book. I am also grateful to others who commented on selected sections: Frederick Chen, Lance Cousins, Angie Cantwell, and Robert Mayer, and also to the publisher's anonymous reviewers, who provided useful feedback at an early stage. Errors and shortcomings remain my own.

INTRODUCTION

HOW PERENNIAL ARE THE BASICS OF BUDDHISM?

A Buddhist friend of mine commented, on hearing that I was writing on the Basics of Buddhism, that the task must be utterly different from writing on many other academic subject areas. For Buddhism, the 'Basics' are constant, he reasoned, quite different from a subject such as Sociology, which changes all the time. He had a good point: as in most religions, in their attitudes to their spiritual heritage, Buddhists hold that the Buddha Dharma, the essential truths revealed by the Buddha, are timeless and unchanging. These teachings will certainly be explored in this book, but it is quite likely that the Basics as presented here will look at least a little different from how the Basics might have looked thirty years ago – or indeed, how they might look in thirty years' time. Why should this be so?

One reason is the state of Buddhist Studies as an academic discipline as opposed to Buddhism as a religious path. The teachings may change little, but our knowledge and understandings of them change and develop. In the early twentieth century, beyond its Asian heartlands, knowledge of Buddhism was sparse. The work of translating the major collections of texts into European languages was in its infancy, and nineteenth-century archaeological discoveries in India had just begun to uncover evidence that allowed glimpses of the early history of Buddhism. It was not until the second part of the twentieth century that Buddhist Studies began to flourish in various university departments throughout Western countries, not only in the relative obscurity of specialist schools for classical 'Oriental' languages, but in Religious Studies, Anthropology,

Philosophy, and Asian Studies. Much has been achieved – but there are many more discoveries to be made, historical understandings to be clarified, more of the extensive textual corpus to be edited and translated, as well as the social and practice dimensions of Buddhist communities to be further explored. The picture we now have of the Basics of Buddhism has developed a good deal, and it is inevitable that that picture will be further added to, and perhaps even transformed by those additions.

Moreover, it is not only the expansion of knowledge in the subject area that is responsible for our changing understandings. Modern academic work proceeds within a wider field in which the focus and the framing of the material changes in response to the academic climate. This is partly a result of advances and developments in academic research, and also of attitudes and interests beyond the university ivory tower. For instance, a generation ago, few people would have expected the issue of gender to be discussed in a book on the Basics of Buddhism, but now, few would write on a major religion without some reference to gender roles! Thus, the Basics as considered here will to some extent reflect current thinking and interests in Buddhist Studies, while not neglecting the central preoccupations of Buddhists themselves.

A rather more fundamental reason why the Basics may not be *quite* so unchanging as they initially appear, is that timeless 'truths' nonetheless manifest or are revealed at specific historical moments. Even the most conservative Buddhist traditions historically accepted additions to their canonical corpus after the earliest discourses and rules on monastic conduct were collected together, and openness to commentarial literature continued for many centuries. In the Mahāyāna Buddhist tradition – as we shall see – textual revelation remained active in India and some traditions preserved the practice of revealing new texts in other Asian countries. This seems to have happened in early Chinese Buddhism, and is still witnessed in Tibet.

BOX 1: THE MAHĀYĀNA

The Mahāyāna ('Great Vehicle') Buddhist tradition first developed during the first century BCE and the first centuries CE. It accepted the earlier Buddhist scriptures as 'Buddha Word', and much of the early

Buddhist heritage of teaching and practice, but it also recognised new texts, the Mahāyāna sūtras/discourses, as scripture, and it gave a central place to the teachings in these texts, which we will examine later. Mahāyāna scriptures continued to be revealed for much of the following millennium, and Mahāyāna scholars made significant contributions to Buddhist philosophy. The Mahāyāna did not, however, develop its own monastic order as such. In India, monks following Mahāyāna traditions might be found within the monasteries of the early Buddhist orders. Later, and internationally (with the exception of Japan), where monasteries have Mahāyāna affiliations, monks still maintain the rule of conduct of one or another of the early Buddhist traditions.

The Buddhist scriptural heritage is vast. It does not consist of a single book or even a few volumes, but of a number of huge many volumed collections, each preserved by one or another Buddhist tradition. The diverse and dynamic nature of the textual heritage may be easily forgotten given that most Buddhist schools closed their canons long ago, but the principle that wisdom may manifest afresh has never been altogether eclipsed in Buddhism. In the contemporary context of rapid social change, political and economic challenges facing traditional institutionalised Buddhism, and increasing international cultural exchanges, there has been much re-thinking and re-working of the Buddhist heritage. How Buddhism changes, evolves, and re-presents its 'basics' is as interesting as how its core interests and assumptions persist.

BUDDHISM TODAY: A SKETCH

According to modern research, the Buddhist tradition began in North-east India in the fifth century BCE. It developed and diversified over time within its original homeland, until it declined for various reasons, including the hostility of some Hindu kings and the Islamic takeover of international trade. Except in the far south where Buddhism lingered slightly longer, the remaining Buddhist monasteries were destroyed by waves of Muslim invaders from the tenth to the thirteenth centuries CE. By the time its last institutions collapsed, however, it had been firmly established in many other Asian countries, having begun its internationalisation by the third century BCE, when the emperor Aśoka did much to encourage and promote its expansion. Different areas in Asia received Buddhist teachings at different times and from different Buddhist traditions, and varying political and social contexts in the recipient countries also sometimes led to the sponsorship of one group of Buddhists at the expense of others. Since the Buddhist order had always been decentralised in organisation, and very early in Buddhist history, different lines of monastic descent began to preserve their scriptural collections separately, there was little to integrate the international Buddhist community. Thus, we have a situation in which quite different Buddhist traditions thrived in different countries, often (despite some notable exceptions) with little communication between them. Western scholars once used to speculate that national cultural characteristics made one form of Buddhism more popular in one country than another, or that certain forms of Buddhism are somehow more inherently attractive to wider groups of people than others, and that this would account for the particular spectrum of Buddhist beliefs and practices in different areas. There is, however, little evidence to substantiate such ideas. Historical accident, or particular historical events with their own complex causal explanations – such as particular kings promoting specific traditions for their own reasons – are entirely sufficient to explain the patterns of religious affiliation across Asia. But an added ingredient to this picture is that the various received traditions were then further developed or adapted in the regions where they became rooted. Innovation did not only take place through textual revelation. As a 'living religion', practice traditions were adapted and developed, so for instance, there are a great many styles of Buddhist chanting in Asian countries. For our purposes, three points of significance follow:

- The Buddhist traditions that survived into modern times reflect some but not all of the historical strands of the religious heritage.
- These traditions may appear, at least on the surface, very different, with different religious languages, texts, monastic conventions, and popular practices.
- This apparent diversity does not necessarily represent dissension or dispute between traditions, but rather, different historical trajectories of separate lines of descent.

Thus, we should avoid imputing sectarian hostility between traditions which have adhered to contrasting beliefs or practices. To give just one example, it is often said that Mahāyāna Buddhism disputed with or is opposed to Theravāda Buddhism – the two major forms of Buddhist affiliation which have survived today, about which we shall say more in this book. Yet when the Mahāyāna developed in Northern India and in Central and East Asia in the early centuries CE, Theravāda Buddhism was already based far away in Ceylon (modern Sri Lanka), and it did not take a central role in Buddhism's evolution in the northern areas. In so far as the Mahāyāna developed an identity in opposition to non-Mahāyāna doctrine, its debating partners were principally of the Sarvāstivāda tradition, which later died out as a separate order, although it left its mark in the monastic code used in Tibet and in the philosophy curriculum studied by Mahāyāna Buddhists. And the Theravāda had earlier rejected some of the Sarvāstivāda doctrines which became the butt of Mahāyāna critiques.

BOX 2: THE THERAVĀDA

The Theravāda (the 'Tradition of the Elders') developed from one of the principal ancient Buddhist orders, and it sees itself as in direct continuity from the earliest Buddhist community. It preserves the only surviving complete corpus of early scriptures in an ancient Indian language, Pāli. It also draws on later commentarial works, including those of Sri Lankan scholars during the first millennium CE.

So, while we need to be aware of diversity, we also need to be aware that the major extant Buddhist traditions do not represent direct parallels to the historical schisms in Christianity or Islam. They are not equivalents to a unified Christian Church separating into Eastern and Western Churches, nor of Western Christianity dividing into Roman Catholicism and Protestantism, nor of Islam splitting into Sunni and Shi'ah traditions. Buddhism has had its historical schisms, but the fault lines do not quite correspond to the major traditions today, and furthermore, doctrinal differences did not always translate into separate institutional or monastic affiliations.

MAJOR BUDDHIST TRADITIONS

The diverse forms of Buddhism, which have survived into recent times, can mostly be categorised into three major regional groupings. None are unified into single hierarchical structures, but all have features which integrate them internally and make them distinctive in relation to each other. These groupings are:

(1) Southern Buddhism, found in Sri Lanka and South-east Asian countries, particularly Burma, Thailand, Cambodia and Laos. The main thread holding this group together is Theravāda Buddhist texts and practice. Theravāda Buddhism derives from one of the ancient Indian schools of Buddhism (see Text Box 2).
(2) Northern Buddhism, practised in Tibet and the surrounding Himalayan areas, and in other areas where Buddhism spread from Tibetan sources, such as parts of Central Asia, principally Mongolia. The Buddhism of this branch derives from later Indian Buddhism especially of the Pāla dynasty (Bengal, eighth–twelfth centuries CE), incorporating Buddhist monastic scholarship, Mahāyāna (see Text Box 1) and tantric traditions (see Text Box 3). It preserves large collections of scriptural and commentarial texts in Tibetan, including a comprehensive set of translations from Sanskrit sources as well as a vast indigenous literature.
(3) East Asian Buddhism, practised in East Asian countries: China, Taiwan, Korea, Japan, Vietnam, and in other countries with substantial ethnic Chinese populations. East Asian Buddhism mainly derives from the Mahāyāna traditions which were established in China in the early centuries CE, although the textual heritage in Chinese includes earlier Buddhist scriptures and a few tantras.

BOX 3: BUDDHIST TANTRIC TRADITIONS

Tantric traditions built on early Buddhist adaptations of ancient Indian magical rites using sacred syllables in Sanskrit. In Mahāyāna sūtras, strings of such syllables were used to grant protection or to epitomise the teachings. From around the seventh century CE, sacred Buddhist texts called *tantras*, taught a new form of Buddhism which used such sacred syllables or *mantras* as techniques for gaining Enlightenment. Parallel to similar developments in other Indian religions, tantric Buddhism (also called the *Mantra Vehicle*) makes use of visualisation, mantra recitation, and ritual meditations to transform ordinary experience into an enlightened wisdom display.

In the contemporary period, globalisation is making a significant impact on this general classification. One striking feature of recent times has been cultural exchange between Western and Asian countries, which has included the expansion of Buddhism in the West, along with Western influences acting on Buddhism in the East. But if on the surface less remarkable, perhaps of greater significance to Buddhism has been the increasing interplay and exchange which the traditional Asian Buddhist groups have had with each other. For instance, we find Theravāda Buddhism becoming established in Nepal, and Tibetan Buddhism expanding in Hong Kong and Taiwan. This does not simply indicate that each geographical area is becoming more varied, but more importantly, that the traditionally established groups need to respond to the new alternatives, and the newer groups may need to adapt and re-think their own traditional practices to cater for their new followers. Moreover, not only do we witness different traditions teaching and practising in the same area, but interchanges also include the study and training of Buddhists of one tradition in the monasteries and countries of another.

Other significant modifications to the classification today occur due to the development and expansion of all manner of new Buddhist organisations, especially in urban areas. In part, this reflects the weakening (or even breakage) of ties between secular socio-political and traditional religious structures and, in part, it reflects the ongoing adaptations of Buddhism to modern urban life. Some new organisations may innovate merely in terms of greater orientation to lay Buddhist practice than their traditional counterparts, coupled with selective choices in drawing on traditional material. But other new organisations may reflect postmodern trends to 'mix and match' religious teachings, and find their inspiration in new mixes of the Buddhist heritage, or even of Buddhist and non-Buddhist spiritual traditions. Buddhism in the West also varies from explicit attempts to construct a specific tradition outside its geographical base, to spiritual organisations integrating Buddhist ideas and practices culled from many different traditional sources. Nonetheless, the threefold categorisation remains generally valid, and it is useful in understanding the derivation, affiliations and religious orientations of specific Buddhist organisations today.

WHAT THE BUDDHA DID *NOT* TEACH: MISCONCEPTIONS ABOUT BUDDHISM

PRIOR 'KNOWLEDGE'

I have often found that new undergraduate students may find the initial stages of Religious Studies courses more intellectually challenging than those of degrees in Anthropology, with which I am also familiar. At first sight, this might seem surprising: most Religious Studies students arrive at university furnished with considerable experience of studying Religion in a non-confessional manner at school, and many have qualifications in the subject. Even mature students, who may have little or no background in the academic study of Religion, come to the subject with relevant life experiences and may be quite widely read in the subject area. In contrast, beginning Anthropology students may never have studied the subject formally before, and may arrive at university with rather vague ideas about what it entails. Yet, as useful as the background knowledge which Religious Studies students bring to their studies may be – and there is no doubt that it *is* helpful to begin university study with prior knowledge of the subject one is embarking upon – it may also be necessary to unravel and re-think some of the ideas one has picked up along the way. Even professional academic researchers are not immune from mistaken assumptions. I sometimes suddenly discover that a specific piece of 'knowledge' I have, which I may have learnt and intellectually internalised when I first became interested in Buddhism as a teenager, is quite simply wrong, and I need to re-examine the facts.

A LIGHT-HEARTED ALLEGORY

For Religious Studies students, and especially those studying Asian religions, there are additional hazards. We find some rather misleading widely held social views about what religions in general, and Asian religions in particular, are about, coupled with the understandable tendency for school education to seek to identify key areas of study which are uniform across all religious traditions. Let us imagine the hypothetical example of a community of people, say, of Chinese descent, who have preserved Chinese Confucian traditions which focus on family lineages and ancestor veneration. Suppose they have had little historical exposure to other religions, and their school educators wish to introduce children to Christianity in a sympathetic manner which draws links between the familiar and the foreign tradition. They may go through the Bible, selecting whatever references they can find to the respecting of ancestors – perhaps Abraham's family lineage might make a good start, and the recital of Jesus's family line of descent in the opening sections of Matthew's Gospel would seem especially promising. No doubt the commandment to honour parents can also be given prominence in presentations of Christianity. Fine – but will this give the pupils a good appreciation of Christianity's main concerns? Probably not. Let's now add another ingredient to our example. Suppose Christian groups have been active in our community of Chinese descent over the last fifty years or so. In today's world, the Christian movements which have most success may not represent the 'mainstream' Christian Churches, but rather a select few breakaway groups, who may have their own distinctive beliefs or practices. Those who speak for traditional Church authorities may at best be seen as neither of greater nor lesser weight than the leaders or spokespersons of the newer Christian groups. Moreover, even those representing the larger Christian Churches are busily attempting to adapt and reinterpret or modernise their practices for the benefit of their new believers, many of whom are entirely convinced that their understandings reflect true Christianity. Under such circumstances, it would be hardly surprising if members of our hypothetical group were to gain ideas about Christianity which would not be very accurate or representative of Christianity as a whole.

CONTEMPORARY UNDERSTANDINGS OF BUDDHISM

Now, I am not suggesting that this hypothetical scenario is an exact parallel to the fate of knowledge about Buddhism in the West! It exaggerates certain tendencies within a far more complex picture, in which we also have balanced and sensitive presentations of the Buddhist tradition, serious scholarship on Buddhist texts, and increasing engagement with Buddhist practice traditions. The point is simply that there are bound to be some distortions in portrayals of a religion representing a small minority in the West, which none-theless has been of long, extensive, and profound influence in Asian societies.

A generation ago, there were very few accurate books in English concerning the Buddhist tradition, and even fewer which were accessible to the educated general public as well as those specialising in what was then seen as Oriental studies. Now, in contrast, there are many excellent books available on a variety of Buddhist studies topics, including useful academic introductions and surveys of Buddhism. Much encouraged by the marvellous work my mentors and colleagues in the subject were producing, from the early 1990s, I designed introductory courses on Buddhism, naively confident that the reading materials I recommended were first class, and that students could hardly go wrong. Why then did I find myself continuing to face essays which reiterated various misconceptions certainly not to be found in any of the books on their reading lists? No doubt some students had failed to attend classes or to read the suggested books, but conscientious students were not exempt from the misleading statements. Many generated colourful mixes of prior 'knowledge' with the new ideas they were meeting in the lectures and textbooks. Finally, I concluded that no matter how good the sources one uses, there is no option but to tackle explicitly the misleading ideas about Buddhism which have somehow permeated popular understandings of Buddhism in the West. Thus, where appropriate in this book, I outline the limitations of certain commonly held ideas I have come across, as well as exploring more nuanced understandings of the material.

EXAMPLES OF BUDDHISM MISCONCEIVED

To give two brief examples: I have mentioned above that Mahāyāna Buddhism is often presented as though it were starkly opposed to Theravāda Buddhism. Presumably, the principal basis for this view is well-meaning school educators or perhaps the popular media, oversimplifying from an observation that the two are different. Unfortunately, rather than inspiring some understanding of diversity within Buddhism, we may end up with caricatures of selfish Theravāda monks interested only in their own Enlightenment – when in fact, practices generating love and compassion are central in Theravāda training, and the role of the community of monks includes responsibilities towards the laity. Conversely, we may encounter misleading ideas about Mahāyāna practitioners, perhaps focused solely on helping others or on worshipping buddha figures, apparently with no thought of serious spiritual endeavour. Of course, ideals are not always lived up to, yet the main thrust of the principal Mahāyāna teachings concerns the tireless development of both wisdom and compassion, and of these, it is wisdom which alone can make compassion effective and ultimately transcendent.

A rather different example is the notion that Buddhism represents some kind of wonderful vision of spiritual evolution, in which even tragic events may all be somehow intended as teachings to inspire us to ever greater wisdom. In this kind of idea, there is perhaps a blend of Theosophy – a mystical movement which had some impact on early Western presentations of Buddhism – and a certain strand of New Age thinking. But all mainstream Buddhist traditions take the view that it is all too easy to regress and to be reborn with less favourable capacities and conditions. Moreover, the more common Buddhist view is that there is no marvellous divine plan but simply the workings of cause and effect, tending towards unhappy results. Thus, the aim of the spiritual path is to cut the chain of causal links and gain liberation from this sorry state of affairs.

Perhaps some readers may have concerns that they will find here a cold academic approach delighting in disabusing them of any notions they may have of links between Buddhist ideas and practices and contemporary interests such as New Age spirituality or peaceful resolution of conflicts or environmentalism. I will certainly seek to avoid spurious comparisons for which we have little evidence but I rather hope that the presentation will provide food for thought about how the Buddhist heritage might be built on in the future, and which chords of contemporary culture it might chime with (or indeed, is already engaging with). It is not for an academic to dictate what people of the present and future may make of Buddhism and where they will take it – this is something which is dynamically developing as we move further into the twenty-first century, and the interplay between religious tradition and modern culture is fascinating to observe. But first we must seek to understand what the religious heritage is in its own terms.

A UNIFYING BUDDHIST PRACTICE: GOING FOR REFUGE TO THE THREE JEWELS

The most obvious feature binding Buddhists of different traditions and persuasions is their commitment to the Three Jewels, the *Buddha*, the *Dharma* and the *Sangha*. The main initiation rite into the Buddhist faith is the ritual *Going for Refuge* to the Three Jewels in the presence of a Buddhist monk or teacher. The regular repetition of the Refuge formula, recited three times, is also used on a regular basis as a preliminary for Buddhist practice of various kinds. It may be proceeded by removing the shoes and entering a temple or shrine-room, making three prostrations before a Buddha image, arranging offerings such as flowers and small bowls of water representing the offerings given to a guest in ancient India, and lighting candles and incense. Generally the formula is recited while sitting on the ground, with the hands held up, palms together in respect.

THE REFUGE FORMULA

I go for Refuge to the Buddha,
I go for Refuge to the Dharma,
I go for Refuge to the Sangha.

As one might expect of such a central and ubiquitous religious act, there are many levels of symbolism and meaning embodied in this ritual formula, and we will unpack these meanings as we progress with the book. To begin with the simplest, the *Buddha* is the Enlightened or Awakened One, the Teacher who is considered to have attained the ultimate realisation and liberation from worldly existence. The *Dharma* is the teaching set forth by the Buddha, the path to the ending of suffering and the attainment of the ultimate peace of Nirvāṇa or Enlightenment. The *Sangha* is the noble community, those of advanced and irreversible spiritual understanding, who can serve for inspiration and guidance in following the Buddha's teaching.

In *Going for Refuge*, homage is paid to the Three Jewels and respect should thereafter be shown to symbols of the Three Jewels. For instance, Buddha images are one symbol of the Buddha, Buddhist texts represent the Dharma, while the monastic community represents the Noble Sangha. Thus, all these objects should be treated with respect and religious devotion. *Going for Refuge* is generally linked with commitment to the basic Buddhist ethical precepts, about which we will say more later. They may be recited following on from the Refuge formula.

The act of *Going for Refuge* represents a statement of faith: an affirmation of confidence in the Three Jewels as worthy of reliance, as a refuge providing a unique kind of support for one's ultimate spiritual welfare. In so far as any universal definition of a 'Buddhist' may have applicability, *Going for Refuge* distinguishes those who follow the Buddha's teaching from those who do not.

THE NATURE OF THE REFUGE COMMITMENT

To what extent is this commitment exclusive and final? In general, Asian religious traditions do not always demand such strict and exclusive adherence as historical Christianity, Islam and Judaism have tended to do. Early Buddhism grew up in a plural religious environment, where there were many different religious paths on offer. Undoubtedly, the early Buddhist tradition sought to promote the uniqueness and superiority of the Buddha and his teaching, and the early Buddhist texts give some sense of the rivalries between different spiritual paths and how the Buddha distinguished his teachings from those of the teachers of other groups. Rivals were not always dismissed as teaching entirely false or misleading doctrines, however. In some cases, alternative spiritual paths might be considered to have some benefits, although not to lead to the ultimate truth which the Buddhist teachings could illuminate. The impression one receives is of the development of a core group of the highly committed, Buddhist monastics and devoted lay supporters, against the backdrop of a larger community, who might make offerings to and receive teachings from Buddhist monks on some occasions and other spiritual practitioners on other occasions.

Multiple religious affiliations were less common in Asian countries where Buddhism became the dominant religious tradition, such as in Thailand or Tibet. Nonetheless, in many parts of Asia where Buddhism spread, Buddhism was not necessarily the only spiritual path and, quite often, different religious traditions were considered to have something to offer in different contexts. For instance, in China, Buddhism became established alongside the indigenous traditions of Confucianism and Daoism. In some religious practices, features of all three might be blended, while each tradition was also considered to have its special expertise in particular types of practices. Thus, Buddhist monks might be called in to perform rituals for the dead, even by those not otherwise practising Buddhism. Even in more clearly Buddhist countries such as Thailand and Tibet, folk religious traditions might be used to deal with some everyday problems, such as troublesome spirits apparently causing ill health. From a Buddhist viewpoint, there need not be a contradiction between such alternative sources of recourse in times of trouble and the Refuge commitment. A distinction is made between the concerns of the spiritual path and those of worldly affairs. In worldly life, many objects may become one's 'refuge' – inevitably, one may have dependence on parents and relatives, on material supports, or indeed, in traditional Asian cultures, on local gods. Yet, unlike the Three Jewels, none of these objects are considered to provide ultimate Refuge from the sufferings of old age, sickness and death, and to lead to spiritual liberation and lasting peace. Having *Gone for Refuge* to the Three Jewels, it is not considered appropriate to take other objects as ultimate sources of solace. The ideal Buddhist may renounce entirely all other 'refuges', yet such a level of commitment is not generally demanded of all.

There is also the possibility of *Going for Refuge* for specific occasions or different periods of time. In today's world, where international spiritual seekers may wish to try out Buddhist meditation for a period, Buddhist teachers may teach and support such practice in a context in which the meditator *Goes for Refuge* for the period of the meditation retreat. A rather more usual manner of *Going for Refuge*, however, is that it should represent a life-long commitment. A much longer period is often envisaged, especially in Mahāyāna contexts. The

Refuge commitment may be made with the intention that one will continue to *Go for Refuge* throughout this and all future lifetimes, until Enlightenment is attained. It may seem rather unrealistic to make such an aspiration if one is an ordinary mortal unlikely to retain clear recollection of the Refuge commitment in future lives! Nonetheless, Indian religious traditions tend to assume that sincere aspirations for positive good can in themselves create a beneficial impact of quite incredible force, such that miracles may even manifest as side effects. Thus, a sincere aspiration to *Go for Refuge* for all future lives may be considered to have a powerful effect on one's continuum of consciousness, such that it will become possible to recover the connection with the Buddha's teaching again and again.

Other benefits may also be anticipated from the commitment. *Going for Refuge* is often explained as a powerful protective force, which may support the individual throughout their life, as well as providing spiritual sustenance beyond this life. Just what the Three Jewels are, and why they are considered to have such effects on an individual who makes the Refuge commitment, is a question we will be exploring throughout the book.

NAVIGATING TECHNICAL TERMS

Readers unfamiliar with Asian religions beginning the study of Buddhism often have difficulties with the many technical terms that confront them. There is no way that a serious teacher can dispense with a technical vocabulary altogether. A religious system packs much symbolic shorthand into its key concepts and practices, and it would be inconceivable to gain more than the most superficial understanding without tackling these code words. For instance, in Christianity, words such as the Resurrection, Justification, the Eucharist, have special senses and implications which the sincere student has no choice but to penetrate. The student is therefore best advised to familiarise themselves with the key terms.

TECHNICAL TERMS IN TRANSLATION

One way to ease the difficulties for an English speaker is to find appropriate English equivalents for the Buddhist terms concerned. Thus, we may speak, as above, of the *Three Jewels* or *Going for*

Refuge, using ordinary English words to indicate the specific meanings they carry in Buddhism. However, this is not always possible, and nor does it entirely solve the problems for students. Some terms have no obvious literal equivalents in English, and in any case, finding agreement on translation in an international context of independent scholars and separate communities of Buddhists would seem a hopeless task. Even in the case of the Three Jewels, some translators prefer to use the Triple Gem. A long-time student of Buddhism who was recently reading a translation of a Tibetan text, asked me who the Three Precious Ones were. The English translator had translated literally the Tibetan equivalent term for the Three Jewels, and arrived at a new English term. This was admirable for communicating the Tibetan connotations of the term, but rather confusing for the international student of Buddhism! In the case of the Three Jewels, despite alternative translations, it seems to make sense to use English. But where a term, such as *Dharma*, does not have an ordinary literal meaning at all, and carries multiple religious connotations, it would seem preferable to retain the Asian word, rather than to attempt an inadequate translation, such as Teaching, Doctrine, Truth, Law or Norm, all of which have been used by various translators, but cannot hope to do full justice to the concept. So, how is the student of Buddhism to get to grips with the Asian words without becoming baffled or overwhelmed?

SANSKRIT AND PĀLI TERMS

The problem for students is not merely a matter of unfamiliarity with foreign words: there are two particular reasons for confusion, and the wary student, aware of these, can avoid pitfalls in understanding, and gain confidence in navigating the technical vocabulary.

The first reason for confusion is that the most commonly used terms in international Buddhist Studies derive from two closely related Indian languages, that is, Sanskrit and Pāli. Buddhism did not develop an internationally recognised sacred language: on the contrary, the emphasis of much Buddhist teaching is precisely that one does not need to have access to a special ritual or mystical vocabulary in order to understand the basic truths Buddhism teaches. The early Buddhist scriptures make use of ordinary language, of simple reasoning and encouragement to contemplate the teachings to test their truth for oneself. Thus, there was no problem in principle with preserving the scriptures in different languages. As mentioned above, Pāli is an ancient Indian language, once spoken in an area of Northern India where the early Buddhist teaching thrived, and the Theravāda Buddhist tradition continues to preserve its early scriptural collection in the Pāli language. As Indian Buddhism developed and took part in wider cultural exchanges with followers of other religious traditions, Buddhist texts began to be rendered into Sanskrit, the language of the religious intelligentsia. Many of the later Indian Buddhist texts were composed in Sanskrit, and Sanskrit became the most widely used international language for Buddhist texts, although Sanskrit texts were further translated into local Asian languages in different areas. Modern studies, much international Buddhist practice, and popular Western interpretations of Buddhism, have generally favoured the use of the Sanskrit terms, such as *Dharma*, *karma* and *Nirvāṇa*, to such an extent that some of these words can be considered to have entered ordinary English vocabulary, even if their original Asian meanings are not fully understood! Yet in the context of Theravāda Buddhism, the Pāli equivalent terms may be used. So, having just begun to understand the Sanskrit words, the student is suddenly confronted with the words, *Dhamma*, *kamma* and *Nibbāna*. So long as one is warned and aware that a given term may be Sanskrit or Pāli, the similarity of the two languages means that it is not too difficult to play a game of guessing the most likely Sanskrit equivalent for a Pāli term (or vice versa), and then checking in a glossary. In this book, I have simplified matters by using Sanskrit for key terms important throughout Buddhism, although the Pāli equivalents used commonly in Theravāda Buddhist practice are noted in the Glossary.

BUDDHIST AND NON-BUDDHIST USAGE OF TERMS

The second reason that students may have trouble with understanding Buddhist terminology is that some of the same terms may be used in other Indian religions, but with quite different connotations in the other religions. One needs to be aware that the terms may not always mean quite the same thing. Again, the term *Dharma* has rather different senses in Hinduism and in Sikhism. In fact, just as early Christianity re-defined key concepts of the Hebrew religious tradition, early Buddhism seems deliberately to have taken up much of the religious and ritual vocabulary of the culturally dominant tradition of the time, and re-fashioned it in new ways. If one has prior knowledge of ways in which the terms may be used in other Indian religions, however, this can help to inform one's overall understanding of Buddhism. After all, Buddhism grew up in constant contact with, influenced and was influenced by other Indian religious currents. But one needs to remember that the Buddhist use of a term may represent a re-working – or even a lampooning – of a term used in contrasting ways in non-Buddhist contexts.

CHINESE AND TIBETAN TERMS

Finally, a few Chinese and Tibetan terms are used, mostly for Chinese and Tibetan Buddhist schools. Confusion is possible in the case of Chinese because there are different systems for transcribing Chinese into Roman script. I have used the now more standard Pinyin system, but many readers may be more familiar with the older Wade-Giles conventions. Thus, *Tao* (Wade-Giles) is given as *Dao*, *Hua-yen* is given as *Huayan*, and so forth. In the case of Tibetan, exact transliteration is the only way to indicate the Tibetan spelling, so this has been done in most cases. Unfortunately, the spellings sometimes appear unpronounceable to the uninitiated, but the number used has been minimised since Sanskrit equivalents are given for most Buddhist terms. Where a word has entered English vocabulary, such as 'lama' (= Tibetan *bla ma*), or where a place or personal name now has a standard English equivalent (Lhasa, Dalai Lama), these Anglicised forms are used.

THE BUDDHA AND THE ROOTS OF THE BUDDHIST TRADITION

Muslims have rejected the terms Muhammadism/Muhammadans as labels for their religion and its adherents, and these Western categories have now fallen into disuse. Contemporary Buddhists have made less fuss about the terms, Buddhism/Buddhists, even though similar objections could be made about them, and they do not neatly correspond with any Asian Buddhist category. The Buddha-Dharma is one term for Buddhism or Buddhist doctrine, which has universal currency in Buddhist countries (albeit often translated into local languages). Here, as in the Tibetan word for a Buddhist practitioner, which could be translated as a 'Dharma-ist', one who follows the Dharma, the emphasis is on the teaching, doctrine, or path, to which the word Buddha may be added as an adjective to clarify *whose* Dharma is at issue. Yet the fact that Buddhists have not objected violently to the newly invented terms indicates that the figure of the Buddha – the first of the Three Jewels – has a central place in Buddhists' understanding of their religious tradition.

HISTORY AND RELIGIOUS MYTHOLOGY

Buddhism derived from and grew out of the teachings of the historical Buddha, who lived for some eighty years most probably during the fifth century BCE. In modern scholarship, we are interested not only

in how the figure of the Buddha came to be understood or portrayed by the Buddhist tradition, but also in the historical facts
about the Buddha's life and his teachings. We have two problems
here. The first is that this is not where Buddhists themselves would
traditionally begin in seeking to understand the Buddha, and the
second is that our historical knowledge remains limited. First,
Buddhism has developed rich and inspiring hagiographies (religious
biographies) of the Buddha, many of which brilliantly use accounts
of the master's deeds to inspire faith in him as the Enlightened one
of the current world system. They illustrate the pertinent points of
his teachings, as well as generating an ideal model for the spiritual
life. Aspects of these stories have entered also into symbolic and
ritual traditions. Just as sequences from the Gospel accounts of the
ministry of Jesus may adorn Christian Churches, and key events
such as the Baptism and the Last Supper have been immortalised in
the Christian sacraments, so, the principal Acts of the Buddha have
taken on a powerful symbolism in Buddhism, even if the Buddha is
not exactly seen as a saviour figure and nor are his Acts considered
to have saving grace in quite the same way as Christianity teaches
about Jesus.

Given the religious value of the hagiographical stories of the
Buddha's life, we should not be surprised if historical realities have
been considerably re-worked and embellished. This is not simply a
matter of adding in a number of miraculous feats or dramatic
encounters with demons or gods. Modern sensibilities have led to
some new Buddhist presentations of the Buddha's life which may
have been purged of miraculous elements, yet otherwise preserve
the same essential structure. The trouble with this is that apparently
ordinary or plausible events in the stories may be equally constructed or take on symbolic significance to the same extent. For
example, the early texts seem to indicate that the Buddha came
from an elite family in a Republican area, his father perhaps an
elected chief. Yet the later hagiographies have him as a noble
prince, the heir to his father's kingdom, and one who had the
potential either to become a great ruler or an enlightened buddha.
Clearly, by juxtaposing the two alternatives, the story adds to the
drama and it makes it clear that the Buddha's choice to renounce
worldly life did not stem from an unfortunate or unworthy alternative
but was made despite the strongest possible worldly incentives.

Moreover, it demonstrates that in an important sense the Buddha is the religious equivalent of a world ruler, a similar symbolism to Christian associations of Jesus as a king. Unpacking such symbolic connotations of traditional accounts of the Buddha will teach us a good deal about Buddhism, but not necessarily very much about the historical Buddha himself.

Here we meet our second problem: our factual historical sources tell us very little. One academic introductory book on the Buddha begins with a short section on 'the bare bones' of his history. Unfortunately, a skeleton may give few clues about the living human's appearance, let alone his or her personality and abilities. Something is known of the historical context in which the Buddha lived. Archaeological work has helped to give us some understanding of the development and character of early Buddhist shrines and institutions, and critical analysis of early Buddhist texts has enabled some distinction to be made between earlier and later strands. But the fact remains that we are dependent on Buddhist sources in the attempt to build up a picture of the historical Buddha. In addition, early Buddhist texts were preserved orally in the first centuries, so that they were only written down many generations after the Buddha's time. Besides the question mark over their reliability for historical purposes, such memorised scriptures do not tend to include much which might be considered extraneous to the main business of expounding the Buddha's teaching. There are no very early biographies: the earliest were composed on the basis of scattered comments reportedly made by the Buddha where his own experience illustrated some point in the teaching.

Some scholars have appealed to a principle of giving greater weight to stories of incidents which would have been of marginal interest to the religious tradition or which expressed sentiments with which the tradition would have been uncomfortable. If the story or anecdote did not fit well with the developing religious mythology, perhaps it might have been recorded and preserved simply because it was true. However, this reasoning at best increases the plausibility of a limited number of events. Since it focuses on matters considered less relevant by the tradition, by the same token, it is unlikely to help us in understanding the central aspects of the Buddha's life, let alone the early development of the religion. For this, we need to make the best of the available sources, bearing in mind their limits. Besides seeking to place the Buddha in his historical context, we can gain some sense of a likely historical scenario by examining the legacy of the early teachings attributed to the Buddha and the emergence of the monastic order, a then new kind of religious institution which almost certainly bears the imprint of the Buddha's own vision of the religious life. At the same time, examining the fully blown mythology of the Buddha's life can enable us to appreciate what the Buddha became for later generations of his followers and, just as importantly, how the Buddhist tradition has conceptualised the most exemplary spiritual path.

THE SCRIPTURAL SOURCES

The earliest sources on the Buddha's life story available to us are the Pāli canonical 'discourses' of the Buddha, the *sutta*s (= Sanskrit *sūtra*s) and texts on monastic discipline, the *vinaya*. Equivalent texts were preserved by the other early orders, and some of these survive in Sanskrit, but not a full collection. Recently, scholarly work on the Chinese *Āgama*s, a collection of translations of early 'discourses', has been advancing our understanding of the earliest heritage, since the Pāli and Chinese parallel texts can be usefully compared. Discrepancies can identify areas where the textual transmission has been corrupted or where editorial intervention has introduced emendations. But for our purposes here, the early Pāli scriptures are the most accessible materials for the more ancient traditions, while later Pāli texts and texts in other Buddhist languages can help us to understand developments.

THE BUDDHA'S CONTEXT AND HIS OWN CONTRIBUTION

Buddhism is sometimes said to have emerged out of Hinduism, and to have inherited Hindu concepts and practices. However, the Buddha's era was before the development of the philosophical systems of classical Hinduism, the widespread adoption of detailed prescriptions for segregating castes, the popular practices of Hindu temple worship and its associated Epic mythologies, and even the various systems of yoga practices which became distinctive of Hindu ascetic groups. The germs of all these religious features were present, however, and it makes more sense to see Buddhism as growing up alongside other Indian religious groupings including Hinduism. During more than a millennium of Buddhism's presence in the sub-continent, at each stage, it influenced and was influenced by those other religious traditions. In the Buddha's time, there were two main religious contexts against which we can usefully see the Buddha's teaching:

(1) The dominant religious culture in much of the area where the Buddha lived and taught is generally referred to by scholars as *Brahmanism*, based on the heritage of a hereditary religious elite preserving a body of exclusive religious practices and oral scriptures called the *Vedas*. Early Buddhism absorbed a good deal of the religious vocabulary of Brahmanism, although it reinterpreted and in some cases lampooned its concepts and practices. In particular, Brahmanism's ritualism, exclusivity and hereditary principles were rejected for an emphasis on universalist ethical principles and reasoned argument, with acts judged on the basis of the extent to which they reflect virtue and wisdom.

(2) A sub-culture which the Buddha joined when he renounced worldly life, was that of a movement of itinerant ascetic hermits, the *Śramaṇas*. The Buddha is referred to in Buddhist sources as the *Great Śramaṇa* or the Great Ascetic or Renouncer. The 'homeless life' extolled in early Buddhist sources suggests a continued self-identification with the ascetic tradition, and an opposition to the Brahmanical householder model for the religious life. Other Śramaṇa groups included the Jains, who were also successful in the long term and whose emergence was a little earlier than that of Buddhism. Jainism's principal exponent, Mahāvīra, was already known as a famous master when the Buddha was teaching. The Śramaṇa groups shared an ascetic code of conduct, similar ascetic and perhaps yogic disciplines, as well as ethical universalism, spiritual and philosophical experimentation and innovation, with room for individual spiritual seekers regardless of social background. At the same time, the Buddha seems to have distinguished his approach from the wider renouncer movement. The Buddhist monastic order was to represent a 'Middle Way' between the hermit and householder life, with its emphasis on monastics as a community in a close

relationship with lay patrons, and a philosophical approach which was frequently contrasted explicitly with the views of rival ascetic traditions.

The social and economic setting for the new religious movements was one of rapid economic growth in the area of the middle Gangetic plain where the Buddha lived, bringing urban development, alongside social and political change, with the expansion and consolidation of the larger regional kingdoms, and their incorporation of the small-scale republics, which included the Buddha's own homeland. The rise of an urban mercantile class who lacked a stake in the older status quo may have been one reason for Buddhism's success. Trading and other well-to-do urban families provided sponsorship and recruits for the early Buddhist order, and, in the longer term, associations with large-scale trading corporations played an important role in the international expansion of Buddhism. In an environment in which political units were growing and perhaps integrating more diverse populations, the political elite seems also to have been exploring alternative role models for rulers than those specified in Brahmanical sources. The Buddha is reported to have advised rulers on their best strategies for successful rule as well as spiritual well-being suggesting, for instance, equanimity and non-attachment in defeat, along with upright conduct in all circumstances, including restraint and generosity even towards defeated foes.

THE BUDDHA'S LIFE STORY

PREVIOUS LIVES

For the Buddhist tradition, the starting point is innumerable lifetimes in the distant past prior to the Buddha's final birth in the world. A Buddha is one who has fully awakened to the truth of the cycle of life and death, whose Enlightenment has brought final release from that cycle, and who can illuminate the spiritual path he had rediscovered to bring others to the same realisation. An enlightened follower may share exactly the same insight, but a special quality of a Buddha is the ability to go where others in the world concerned have not gone before, and to shine the torch of the spiritual teaching. To perfect the necessary capabilities for such an achievement is considered to take vast periods of time, spent with single-minded dedication to the heroic pursuit of virtue and wisdom. According to the hagiographies which developed along with the Buddhist tradition, the story begins many aeons ago, with the Buddha-to-be as the ascetic Sumedha, setting forth on the path through meeting and being inspired by a Buddha called Dīpaṃkara. On making a firm vow to work for the complete Enlightenment of a Buddha, Sumedha thus became a *bodhisattva*, a being intent on Enlightenment, and Dīpaṃkara recognised the force of his resolve, predicting his eventual Enlightenment in our world system.

This story is known throughout the Buddhist world, as are many of the *Jātaka* tales, a whole class of Buddhist literature consisting of stories of the Buddha-to-be during his previous lives, meeting desperate challenges and adversities with noble determination, wisdom and compassion, thus perfecting the virtuous qualities necessary for the final climax of the spiritual path. These stories, some of which were popular fables derived from non–Buddhist sources, and some which were composed with Buddhist themes in mind, became significant pedagogic tools in Asian Buddhist cultures, expressed not only in story-telling but in temple art and in dramatic performances and operas. The most well-known stories include tales of the *bodhisattva* as an animal king, acting, for instance, to help members of his own species from the machinations of some evil humans, and in the end teaching those humans to reform their ways by his example. The anthropomorphism hardly fits comfortably with modern scientific models of ecology. Nonetheless, contemporary Buddhists interested in animal rights or ecological ethics may justly reflect that such stories highlight a Buddhist approach that living beings share a good deal in terms of their basic emotional impulses, and that creatures may be born in different states in subsequent rebirths, so that human and animal life are not to be seen as wholly separate conditions, nor are animals always to be seen as inherently inferior or less worthy than human lives.

Although the fanciful stories of the Buddha's previous lives are a far cry from the references given by the Buddha in the earliest scriptures of his spiritual journey, they can certainly be seen as an extension of similar attitudes expressed in the early canonical texts regarding the status of a buddha, his attributes and achievement, and the ethical values of Buddhism. The idea of a succession of endless lives predated Buddhism and in an early description of the Enlightenment experience, the Buddha recounts how he surveyed his many previous lives, noting the circumstances and the working of cause and effect in their progression. The Pāli *Dīgha Nikāya*, the Pāli collection of long discourses attributed to the Buddha, contains a teaching in which the Buddha details the life history of a previous buddha, as well as the names of a number of other buddhas and their parents, attendants and principal students. The main force of this discourse, called the *Mahāpadāna Sutta* (DN 14), seems to be the stress on the identical pattern by which buddhas arise in the world, attain Enlightenment, teach and pass away into final liberation.

BIRTH

The traditional hagiographies continue with an account of the bodhisattva's conception and birth, which feature prominently in the pan-Buddhist traditions of the Buddha's Acts, and which are outlined briefly but nonetheless with some flourish, in the early scriptures. This includes the Pāli *Accariya-abbhūta Sutta* in the collection of the Buddha's middle-length discourses, the *Majjhima Nikāya* (MN 123), which gives a list of wondrous happenings marking the birth, and the *Mahāpadāna Sutta* account mentioned above. Here, we find an outline of the pattern of every buddha's life, matching several of the key elements of the specific story which developed in relation to our world's present Buddha. Some Buddhist modernists play down the miraculous components of this account, seeking to focus on core Buddhist teachings and in some cases to contrast Buddhism with Christianity's emphasis on Jesus's miraculous conception and birth. Such a perspective can be seen as a development within an important strand of Buddhism today, but we must not lose sight of historical Buddhism's celebration of the bodhisattva's amazing feats on entering the world.

The full mythological account of what became classified as the first three of the Buddha's twelve Acts, his descent into and birth in our world, begins with his previous birth in the Tuṣita heaven, a divine paradise in which birth is a result of the accumulation of great merits from virtuous deeds, yet this does not imply the level of perfect wisdom or final liberation attained by a buddha. From the Tuṣita heaven, the bodhisattva could survey our world and await the right moment for the descent into his destined final body. When the beings of this world became mature enough for his presence, he entered Queen Māyā's womb, after which she became free from any mental afflictions. A dream of a regal white elephant entering her womb made her aware that she was pregnant, carrying an exceptional child. The bodhisattva was born after ten lunar months while his mother was travelling from her husband's to her own family home for the birth. While she stood, holding onto a blossoming *sal* tree in a grove in Lumbinī, he emerged from her right side, causing her no pain and avoiding any defilement from the birth canal. Although still a newborn baby, he stood upright, took seven steps and scanned the four quarters, proclaiming his status as the eldest of beings and confirming that this would be his final birth. A hermit seer called Asita foresaw the significance of the birth, and came to pay his respects, while admitting sadness for the fact that he himself would pass into a heavenly realm before the Buddha would attain Enlightenment. Brahman astrologers examined the child and identified a full list of auspicious marks indicating that he was a great personage, destined either to be a righteous world ruler or an enlightened buddha. But one young yet saintly brahman realised that the destiny of buddhahood was inevitable, and immediately became an ascetic to prepare himself to receive teachings from the great master. The chief of the group of the Buddha's first five disciples is identified with this young brahman.

It is clear that at the very least, the account of the bodhisattva's 'descent' and birth, portrayed as his first significant Acts, creates a picture of a person of exceptional qualities and super-human abilities. The idea of the special bodily marks most probably derives from an ancient Indian list of signs for recognising a superman. It is found in virtually every version of the story, including the *Mahāpadāna Sutta* description of the features of every buddha, and it is elaborated upon at greater length in another *Dīgha Nikāya* discourse, the *Lakkhaṇa Sutta* (DN 30), which relates the specific marks to the virtuous inner qualities perfected by a buddha-to-be. The content of the list varies in different Buddhist sources, but many remained stable – such as the shining gold complexion, the wheels on the soles of the feet and the palms of the hands, the round protuberance on the head, and tight clockwise curls of hair. Some, such as depictions of the soles of the feet, became symbols of the Buddha, and the first

Buddha images to be used in worship some centuries later, drew on the list to generate imagery in harmony with the tradition. In the Buddha's life story, they indicate the two possible directions which the great person may take, since righteous emperors share these auspicious signs. Later they become a defining feature of a fully enlightened buddha. They remain prominent in later Mahāyāna imagery of celestial buddhas exhibiting subtle radiant qualities perceptible only to advanced bodhisattvas, and versions of them also occur in tantric meditations on buddhas and enlightened deities.

CHILDHOOD AND YOUTH

Many accounts of the Buddha's life say comparatively little about his youth and less about his childhood. The early scriptures made few references to his early years, so there was less for the later biographers to build on in comparison with the main story of how he attained liberation. There is one interesting story, however, which relates directly to his final spiritual goal, and is mentioned in the Pāli *Mahā Saccaka Sutta* in the *Majjhima Nikāya* (MN 36). In this text, the Buddha reflects on the course of his spiritual path, from his decision to renounce worldly life to his Enlightenment. He describes a key turning point when he recognised the uselessness of the severe austerities he had been inflicting upon himself, and began to take nourishment in order to develop the strength and mental clarity to complete the path to awakening. He explains that the recognition came to him in recollecting a spontaneous deep meditative experience which he had had as a child. He had been sitting in a cool place in the shade of a rose-apple tree while his father was working nearby. Calm and at peace, he had entered a state of focused rapture. The adult ascetic reflects that such a blissful and peaceful state which was entirely devoid of any sensual grasping or unwholesome mental conditions, is an appropriate basis for the realisation of Enlightenment. Already in the account, the specific meditative state is referred to as the first of a series of four progressively staged deep absorptions (*dhyāna*s), which are then described as occurring in the first part of the night before the Enlightenment. As we shall see, they have remained important in Buddhist meditation systems.

The hagiographic series of the Buddha's Acts include one on his mastery of all the scholarship, languages, material arts and recreations of the time, including training in warriorship and administrative rule appropriate for his status. It is through his successful feats in an organised competition that he wins the hand of his virtuous and beautiful bride, with whom he is considered to have had good connections in previous lives. The following Act relates to the bodhisattva's enjoyment of marriage and worldly success, culminating in the production of a son, born just on his departure in the early canonical version and later in some of the other versions. The more flowery descriptions include much detail on the delights, such as music and dancing girls, provided by the king to distract the prince from any sober reflections which might incline him to ascetic renunciation.

What is clear, even in the earliest canonical discourses, is that the Buddha-to-be had an early life of wealth and privilege. In an early account given in the *Sukhamala Sutta* of the *Aṅguttara Nikāya* collection of the Buddha's discourses (AN 3.38/39), the Buddha recounts how his father supplied him with the finest clothes and adornments from Varanasi, three lotus pools and three different halls in which to relax in the cooler, hot and rainy seasons, and he comments that even the servants were given good foods. The point is considerably embellished in later hagiographies which portray him as a young prince with a life of indulgence. But perhaps he was rather like spiritual seekers today who may have experienced material well-being and found it wanting. The *Sukhamala Sutta* continues that the Buddha's intoxication with youth, health and life fell away in the light of his reflections on the realities of ageing, sickness and death.

RENUNCIATION

There is a twist to the narrative of the alternative destinies prophesised at birth introduced by a further component given in many of the sources discussing the predictions of the brahmans. When questioned about the two possibilities, the brahmans clarify that the choice to aim for buddhahood will only arise if the prince (in later versions) encounters four signs: an old and a sick man, a corpse, and an ascetic renouncer. The account of the bodhisattva's reflections leading up to his renunciation thus take on the drama of his father's repeated attempts to prevent his meeting with these signs and the irony that the king's actions in the end contribute to the inevitable conclusion. The fact that the prince is so successfully sheltered from life's miseries increases his shock at the discovery of the facts of ageing, sickness and death. That he had experienced the most indulgent excesses of life's pleasures adds to the consequent revulsion when their ultimately unsatisfactory nature is revealed.

Here, the story is seeking to demonstrate the fundamentals of Buddhist teaching and, quite possibly, may well reflect the Buddhist community's earliest understanding of the Master's spiritual journey. The pattern of the sequential witnessing of the four manifestations, while being driven by his charioteer on a series of pleasure trips, is described at some length in the *Mahāpadāna Sutta*, where it is linked to the life story of a previous buddha. Another Pāli text, the *Ariyapariyesana Sutta* of the *Majjhima Nikāya* collection (MN 26), presents the Buddha's reflections on his spiritual path in an account which has been considered by modern academic scholars as likely to be particularly early. Experiencing himself as subject to birth, decay, sickness, death, grief and defilement, the Buddha comments that he realised the futility of further seeking for birth, decay, sickness, death, grief and defilement. Knowing the dangers of these characteristics of life, the noble course of seeking instead for their cessation occurred to him. This, then, was the motive for the momentous decision to renounce the worldly life and work single-mindedly for the total appeasement and cessation of birth and death, and the resultant attainment of peace and Enlightenment. In a passage occurring in both the *Ariyapariyesana Sutta* and also in the *Mahā Saccaka Sutta* referred to above, the Buddha describes himself as having made his decision as a youth with pitch black hair, and against the wishes of his tearful parents, donning yellow robes and leaving the household life.

This brief illustration of the noble search, apparently on the basis of the Buddha's own experiences, does not explicitly contradict the more elaborate descriptions of the bodhisattva's progress. However, some modern academic scholars have suggested that it might cast some doubt on the tradition, well established in other Pāli canonical sources and elsewhere, of the bodhisattva's marriage and the birth of a son, as though as a final temptation to bind him. In some later versions, such as the Pāli *Nidānakathā*, much is made of the Buddha's agonised mental conflict as he prepares to part from his wife and child, assuaged only by the recognition that he could be of greater value to them and others in winning through to spiritual peace. The Buddha's family members and others of the Śākya community apparently became enthusiastic followers soon after the start of the Buddha's teaching career. They feature in the early collections of the Buddha's discourses and monastic discipline, as well as later texts which flesh out the material. His aunt who had been his foster mother appears in the early scriptures, persuading the Buddha to ordain her and found the community of nuns. His wife, who sought to emulate her husband's example and to live like an ascetic after his departure, also became a disciple and was said to have reached sainthood. On the Buddha's initial return to his homeland, his young son was instructed to request his father to transmit to him his inheritance, so that the family succession would be ensured. The Buddha agreed, but took the concept of inheritance to imply spiritual transmission, so he promptly ordained his son, who became renowned for holding and transmitting the order's monastic lineage. One story has it that the Śākya commitment to Buddhism was so total, that when the land was overrun by a neighbouring kingdom, the people put up no violent resistance and were massacred. One wonders about the motivation for preserving an account – whether true or not – in such contrast to other religions' celebrations of their worldly achievements, such as the Muslim notion of 'Manifest Victory', applied to early Muslim political success and expansion. Perhaps the only plausible explanation is in terms of the symbolism of the Buddha's heritage as exclusively focused on the monastic rather than any family lineage.

The story of the 'Great Renunciation', the sixth of the Buddha's Acts, revolves around his growing awareness of the inadequacy of ordinary conditioned existence, given the facts of impermanence and suffering, along with the conviction that the ascetic life could provide an alternative which would bring contentment and peace. In the hagiographic story of the four signs, it is the fourth sign of the happy and undisturbed ascetic, which demonstrates the way out. Some later versions of the story add an altercation with Māra, a tempter-deity or Buddhist devil, personifying ignorance and emotional defilement, who attempts to dissuade the bodhisattva from his decision. The specific temptation dangled before him is the promise that in seven days he would become a universal ruler, a reminder of the opposition or parallel potential suggested by the birth prophecies. Perhaps a further significance is that here the possibilities for worthwhile beneficial involvement in worldly affairs are raised more clearly than in the episodes which focus on the youthful indulgence of the pre-Renunciation life, and the over-shadowing presence of the bodhisattva's father, giving little sense of the rewarding prospects of mature adult responsibilities.

TRAINING AS AN ASCETIC RENOUNCER

The next key event in the narratives is the sequential training under two meditation masters, who are named in early canonical sources, where their meditation systems are described in brief. The first master taught a practice which was said to lead to a state of 'no-thingness', while the second master's system was said to bring the state of 'neither perception nor non-perception'. The description is preserved in both the *Mahā Saccaka Sutta* and the early discourse on the 'noble search' (the *Ariyapariyesana Sutta*) mentioned above. The Buddha reports that in each case he mastered the system, after which the teacher publicly recognised his achievement and offered him a leadership role to the group of followers. However, while recognising the value of the meditation systems, both of which required conviction, persistence, mindfulness, concentration and discernment, he remained dissatisfied, since neither attainment brought liberation from the sorrows of life, so, in each case, he travelled on. After he attained Enlightenment, the *Ariyapariyesana Sutta* notes that it was his two teachers he thought of first when considering who would have the greatest potential to understand the truth he had realised, but he regretfully saw that both had passed away. It is quite likely that these discourses genuinely preserve a record of the teachings received by the Buddha-to-be in his early days as an ascetic renouncer. It may even be that the meditation practices were adopted from these previous teachers and integrated into the Buddhist system as important components of the training. This is clearly how the Buddhist tradition sees it. However, some modern academic scholars have suggested that the story might have been post-Buddhist, constructed as a way of framing these *Buddhist* meditation practices to make it clear that they are valuable but not to be mistaken for the highest training. They are known only from early Buddhist sources and their presentation seems rather formulaic and standardised, to correspond rather precisely to Buddhist categories both of the meditative states and of formless divine realms into which one can be born. It would not be easy to prove the case either way. But certainly, the account would seem to reflect an understanding of the Master's spiritual path stemming from the earliest generation of students.

The *Ariyapariyesana Sutta* proceeds seamlessly from the training under the meditation teachers to arrival in beautiful countryside and the attainment of Enlightenment, but the *Mahā Saccaka Sutta* continues with a graphic description of his experimentations with various techniques of self-mortification. This immersion in austerities became the seventh Act of the hagiographies, said to have taken six years. The focus in many of the eulogised versions is on the bodhisattva's great determination and heroism in his self-imposed discipline. The *Mahā Saccaka Sutta* account makes it clear that he took such austerities to their limit, such that no other ascetic could take them further. His body deteriorated, even the clear bright golden colour of his skin, which is counted as one of the auspicious marks. Finally, he concluded that such physical punishment has no benefit and is in fact detrimental to real spiritual progress, making the body too weak to meditate effectively. Thus, he began to eat again, and this provided strength for the meditations which led to his awakening.

The juxtaposition of the excessive indulgences of the bodhisattva's youth and the excessive asceticism of the period of austerities in the hagiographic accounts is clearly intended to highlight the central Buddhist teaching of the Middle Way. Although the references within the early discourses are more scattered, this was doubtless also the intention in these sources too: the whole point is that neither the self-indulgence of worldly life, nor the self-mortification of asceticism is worthy or profitable, but the valid path is to be found in steering between them. There is some difference in tone, however, between different versions. While the Buddhist model of the spiritual path as a Middle Way may be clear, it is not altogether explicit whether or not the bodhisattva's suffering had been necessary to discover it. The *Mahā Saccaka Sutta* account and, indeed, the phrasing of the teaching classified as his first discourse in which he outlines the spiritual path, would seem to imply the asceticism simply to have been an unprofitable dead-end. Yet as one of the

Acts of the Buddha, there may sometimes be the sense that only the years of unremitting struggle made the final breakthrough possible. This kind of approach may especially be emphasised in Buddhist traditions favouring contemplative meditation which may involve the hardships of a reclusive lifestyle, and the need for perseverance.

ENLIGHTENMENT

The stories surrounding the Enlightenment generally begin with the bodhisattva sensing that he is on the brink of realisation and setting off to take his seat under the Tree of Enlightenment in the place which became known as Bodhgaya, making a firm determination not to rise again until he has won through. One version has it that after taking a nourishing meal of rich milk rice, provided by a lady in fulfilment of a vow of offering to a local deity, he dropped his alms bowl into the Nerañjarā River with the pledge that if his resolution swiftly to attain Enlightenment was valid, then the bowl should float in the wrong direction. Immediately, the bowl was swept upstream against the current. The story is an example of ancient Indian 'truth magic', based on the idea that a pure and righteous aspiration made with truthful determination has the capacity to work miracles. Provided by a brahman with a bundle of *kuśa* grass, a sacred grass used in Vedic ritual, the bodhisattva prepared his seat beneath a pipal tree, and sat in cross-legged meditation posture.

The most dramatic story of what followed concerns the assault of Māra, the Buddhist devil, symbolising attachment and ignorance, which began at nightfall. None of the accounts of the Enlightenment experience as related by the Buddha in the earliest of the discourses refer to Māra's preceding attack, although the *Padhāna Sutta* in the *Sutta-nipāta* of the *Khuddaka Nikāya* (Sn 3.2) consists of a poetic description of Māra's attempts to dissuade the bod- hisattva and of the bodhisattva's resistance, including the identification of troops in Māra's army, such as sensual desire, discontent, hunger and thirst, and his resolution to remain firm. Various parts of the collection of discourses feature other encounters between the Buddha or his disciples and Māra and his circle. A whole division of the Pāli *Samyutta Nikāya* (SN 4) is devoted to Māra and his ingenious distractions, and we meet there Māra's 'daughters', Craving, Disinterest and Passion. It would certainly seem that much of the imagery of Māra's role as the 'evil one' seeking to distract or lead the spiritual seeker astray was developed early. In the later hagiographies, the onslaught is usually begun immediately prior to the Enlightenment, when Māra perceives that his dominion over the world is under threat, that the bodhisattva is about to escape his clutches and will then be able to teach others likewise to gain liberation. There are numerous variations in the tale. Popular elements include Māra confiding his fears to his sons and daughters, an amassing of a huge army darkening the sky, with a thousand-armed Māra appearing at its head, the firing of weapons, none of which can impact on the bodhisattva's meditative absorption, the defeated Māra's resentful challenge, and his final flurry in sending his daughters, who miserably fail in their attempt to charm the bodhisattva from his resolution.

It is Māra's challenge which takes centre stage in many of the narratives and, again, we have hints here of a symbolism of a buddha as an alternative kind of universal ruler. Māra proclaims his own right to rule the world, and challenges the bodhisattva to justify the usurpation of his seat or throne. Refusing to give up his place, the bodhisattva calls the earth as his witness that his long spiritual development over many lifetimes has earned him the right to take the seat of Enlightenment. Touching the earth with his right hand, in some earlier versions the earth itself trembles and acknowledges the claim, while, in what became the more standard account, the earth goddess rises up from the earth and bears witness. Māra's legions are scattered in disarray, and the bodhisattva enters his final contemplations which bring Enlightenment. Versions of this story became so important in the Buddhist tradition that the 'earth-witnessing' gesture with the tips of the right hand fingers stretched down to touch the earth came to symbolise the Buddha's Enlightenment, and to be represented in Buddha images throughout the Buddhist world.

Unsurprisingly, we find many different understandings in the Buddhist tradition about the content of the final enlightening meditations. Even in the oldest canonical literature, slightly different nuances can be found, but the early scriptures, which say little about Māra's assault, have a good deal to say about the Buddha's discoveries. These differing accounts and passing references can be seen as complementary, simply emphasising different aspects of the Buddha's realisation, although some modern academic scholars have analysed them as indicating different voices in the early tradition. However, the most extended descriptions of the Enlightenment experience found in the earliest texts fairly consistently detail the successive attainment of the four deep absorptions, followed by three knowledges. Versions of this account are repeated in a number of early sources, including the *Mahā Saccaka Sutta* mentioned above and the *Bhayabherava Sutta*, also in the *Majjhima Nikāya* collection (MN 4). They are also included in later hagiographic works such as Aśvaghoṣa's *Buddhacarita* of the first to second century CE, preserved in part in Sanskrit and in full in Tibetan and Chinese. According to the Pāli sutta versions, the Buddha recounts how he became physically calm and contented, with the mind single pointed. Then, he dispelled sensual and evil thoughts and experienced the bliss of the first deep absorption. Through further concentration, he rested in the second, and then the third deep absorption, in mindful equanimity, and then dispelling all pleasantness and unpleasantness, the mindful equanimity was purified in the fourth deep absorption. The mind thus focused, undisturbed, pure and free from defilement, he directed the mind in the first watch of the night to the knowledge of his previous births, recollecting the full details of uncountable cycles of births and deaths. In the second watch of the night, he directed his mind to the births and deaths of beings, and perceived not only the innumerable different states in which they arose and passed away, but how these changes were conditioned by the beings' own actions (*karma*). Finally, in the third watch of the night, he attained the third knowledge, by directing the mind to the destruction of craving. Gaining understanding of the process of the arising and ceasing of craving, he knew how to bring craving to an end, ignorance was dispelled and he knew he was released and no longer subject to rebirth. The *Buddhacarita* version adds that in the fourth watch, as dawn was breaking, the Buddha attained the state of omniscience.

TEACHING

For some weeks, the story goes that the Buddha remained in the same vicinity. One tradition preserved in the Pāli texts on the monastic discipline has it that he was visited by two travelling merchants who made him offerings and, recognising his achievement, took refuge in the Buddha and the truth he had discovered, thus becoming the

first Buddhists. At this stage, since the Buddha had not commu-
nicated his teaching, refuge could only be taken in the first two
Jewels since there was no enlightened community. In fact, it seems
that the Buddha had doubts about teaching at all. The story is told
in the early *Ariyapariyesana Sutta* (MN 26), in which the Buddha
reflects that his discoveries are hard to understand, they go against
the stream of most people's understanding, and are not accessible to
those governed by attachment and hatred. Any attempt to teach
such people shrouded in darkness will only bring weariness. At this
point, the Brahmā deity Sahampati intervenes to request the
Buddha to teach, pointing out that some have little dust in their
eyes and the teaching will benefit them and help to remove the
world's suffering. In developed Buddhist doctrine, *turning the wheel
of the teachings (Dharma)* is one of the main roles of a fully enlightened buddha, in contrast to another category of Buddhist saints,
pratyeka-buddhas, who become liberated independently, yet who
only teach minimally. The idea persisted, however, that the
Buddha – and, indeed, any Buddhist teacher – should be requested
to teach, creating the auspicious circumstances in which most can
be gained from the teaching. The imperative to spread the teaching,
important in a religious tradition convinced of the unique value of
its Master's vision, is nonetheless tempered by a caution that the students
should be receptive and the teachings appropriate for them.

In this case, in the absence of the Buddha's former teachers, the
standard account found early and late has it that he thinks of the
group of five fellow ascetic renouncers who had accompanied him
during his self-mortifications, but left him in disgust when he gave
up austerities. Thus, he makes his way to where they are residing in
the game park in present-day Sarnath. At first, they are reluctant to
acknowledge the change in him, but soon they welcome him,
although the *Ariyapariyesana Sutta* version suggests that they repeatedly question him on how he could have come to liberation while
living 'luxuriously'. This account goes on to recount that he was
able to convince them that he had not fallen back into worldly
ways, and taught them over the next period, such that they all
became liberated. The only specific teaching mentioned concerns
the avoidance of the bonds of sensuality but, early on, the Buddhist
tradition came to embed the teaching on the Four Truths of the
Noble Ones into this slot. It fits the narrative development perfectly,

and, indeed, it is most likely that the structure of the contrasting worldly and ascetic lifestyles were played out precisely to illustrate the Middle Way teaching. Thus, the Four Truths are expounded in a discourse classified as the first 'Turning of the Dharma Wheel', the *Dhammacakkappavattana Sutta* in the Pāli *Saṃyutta Nikāya* collection (SN 56.11). Here we meet an important Buddhist symbol, the 'Dharma Wheel', an image of which may be displayed prominently above the entrances of Buddhist temples, often flanked by two deer, representing the deer found in the game park in Sarnath. Put simply, the symbolism relates to the idea that the Buddha's teaching is like a wheel, able to replace and put a stop to the never-ending wheel or cycle of life's miseries. Generally, especially nowadays, the Dharma Wheel has eight spokes for the Noble Eightfold Path (see Chapter 2), which work together rather than in a strictly progressive sequence. There are also again connotations relating to the Buddha as a universal ruler: imagery surrounding the righteous emperor has him as a 'wheel-turning' king, applying socially beneficial justice in the world, and, as mentioned above, the marks of the great personage include wheels – in this case, thousand-spoked – on the soles of the feet (as specified in the *Dīgha Nikāya*'s *Lakkhaṇa Sutta*). In the Mahāyāna traditions, major developments in the teaching, which were thought to indicate quite new directions, were later classified as a second and third 'Turning of the Dharma Wheel', still considered to be associated with the Buddha, in discourses which were not made public at the time. We will hear more about the various 'turnings' below.

For the rest of the Buddha's life, perhaps some forty-five years if the traditional accounts preserve an accurate record of the Buddha's life-span, he had a long and varied teaching career, walking throughout the region, founding a monastic order, gaining many lay sponsors, and teaching apparently up to his final moments. As one can imagine, a wealth of stories surround much of this activity, some of them built into the preserved collections of discourses and books on monastic discipline, often as background to the teaching recorded, and others elaborated in later sources.

MIRACLES

In the hagiographic series of the Buddha's Acts, however, this rich legacy of material is summarised into the 'Turning of the Dharma

Wheel' and his passing away into the 'final Nirvāṇa' or liberation. There are some slight variants, however. In one common version, the Austerities are followed by the three separate Acts of taking of the Seat of Enlightenment, Vanquishing Māra, and Enlightenment. In other versions, these may be merged together, and up to two further Acts are inserted after the Wheel Turning. Both relate to miraculous demonstrations, and they are often linked. The accounts are elaborated in Pāli and Sanskrit commentarial and extra-canonical later sources. The story begins by drawing attention to the restrictions which the Buddha had imposed on his monks from public exhibitions of supernormal powers. Supernormal powers are seen in Buddhist tradition as a side effect of the deep absorptions, but apart from the ability to see directly into past lives and the workings of cause and effect, not in themselves of any value for liberation. They might even become possible distractions and, most seriously, might mislead lay followers. The story has it that non-Buddhist rival groups sought to take advantage of the Buddhist avoidance of shows of miracles, subjecting the Buddha and his monks to ridicule. King Bimbisāra, the king of Magadha, who had become an early disciple, therefore requested the Buddha to accept a challenge to perform miraculous feats, and he did so at the city of Śrāvastī (Pāli, Sāvatthī). There are many variants on the exact miracles performed, including the creation of numerous emanations all teaching the Dharma, jewelled terraces in the air on which he walked, waters flowing from his upper body and flames from his lower body. All versions have it that the rival groups were soundly defeated, and the general populace suitably impressed and drawn to the Buddha's teaching. In the plural Indian religious environment in which Buddhism developed, it was no doubt important for the Buddhists to emphasise that rules forbidding monks from magical displays did not reflect their lack of ability but, rather, restraint in its use.

Sometimes just preceding, and sometimes just following the Śrāvastī miracles, comes an account of the Buddha's visit to and sojourn in the Trāyatriṃśa (Pāli, Tāvatimsa) heaven. Here he spent a rains retreat period – a three-month rainy season retreat in which monks are advised to stay in one place and focus on intensive practice. The Buddha was supposed to have taught the gods at this time, and, most significantly, his mother, who had been reborn in a divine realm, was able to attend and attain a high spiritual state.

Depictions of this Act generally focus on the descent back to the human world at the end of the retreat, accompanied by gods and walking down a jewelled ladder created especially by the gods. Here, the focus is not so much on the miraculous dimension as such, but the Buddha's continuing positive communication with the Brahmanical gods, who are shown as supporting his every step and recognising his pre-eminence.

THE FINAL NIRVĀṆA

The final Act of the Buddha is his passing away or *parinirvāṇa*, the final nirvāṇa, when the last vestiges of earthly or even of heavenly life are left behind for the peace of final liberation. The earliest traditions on the last days, such as the Pāli *Mahāparinibbāna Sutta* found in *Dīgha Nikāya* (DN 16), are already highly mythologised, including, for instance, an episode in which Māra once again visits the Buddha, this time to persuade him to pass away. Without such agreement, the story goes that a Buddha can live for an aeon. The Buddha gives his faithful attendant, Ānanda, three opportunities to request him to remain for longer, but the unfortunate Ānanda fails to appreciate what is required of him, and the moment is lost. Again, we have the perennial Buddhist theme of the importance of the student requesting the master rather than expecting to receive his presence and teachings passively. The distressed Ānanda, however, is reminded that everything is finally impermanent, even the life of a Buddha. He is reassured that his long dedicated attendance will bring the positive result of his being able to become enlightened swiftly after the Buddha has passed away. Perhaps the most important element of the mythology of the closing days is the emphasis on the continuity of the Buddhist Order. Māra's argument, to which the Buddha assents, is that the Buddha has successfully established all the groups of his students – monks, nuns, laymen and laywomen – firmly and irreversibly on the spiritual path to liberation, with the intent and abilities correctly to pass on the teachings so that the Dharma will be secure. The point is underlined in the Buddha's final scene with his students, in which he points out that the teachings and code of discipline which he has established will serve as their teacher and authority. On questioning them on whether they have any doubts or queries, they are all silent, at which the Buddha confirms that the whole assembly has no doubts concerning the Three Jewels, and have irreversible spiritual attainment, and he encourages them to persevere. Entering into deep meditation, he goes through the progressive states of deep absorption, and passes away from the fourth deep absorption, the same absorption from which he became Enlightened.

The imagery mentioned in the text, and repeated in later sources also, is of the Buddha reposing on his right side, between two *sal* trees, blossoming out of season, a motif echoing his birth. In much later temple art and statues, the famous posture is depicted in images representing the final nirvāṇa. The scripture also provides a mythological charter for Buddhist traditions of devotional remembrance of the Buddha, traditions which were no doubt established early. It is the Buddha himself in the text who recommends pilgrimage to the four sacred places, where he was born, enlightened, turned the Dharma Wheel, and passed into the final nirvāṇa. The final part of the text discusses the Buddha's cremation and sacred remains, which were divided into eight portions allotted to different groups, all of whom constructed large reliquaries known as *stūpa*s to house the relics. Thus, the *stūpa* as a symbol of the Buddha, the Buddha's mind, or the final nirvāṇa, and the cult of honouring *stūpa*s and relics was said to have been initiated from the moment the Buddha himself passed away.

NAMES AND TERMS FOR THE BUDDHA

Besides the technical terms, *bodhisattva* and *buddha*, applied to the Buddha before and after the Enlightenment, respectively, various other names and titles may be used. The Buddha is frequently referred to as the renouncer Gautama (Pāli Gotama), in the early texts, and this would seem to be the name by which he was known in the wider community. His own students, however, do not generally address him by the name, since this would be considered disrespectful. They more usually use the honorific title found throughout Buddhist texts, of *Bhagavān*, which has been translated variously, such as 'Blessed One' or 'Venerable Lord'. The name Siddhārtha (Pāli Siddhattha), meaning Wish-fulfilled, is mentioned in later hagiographies, such as the Pāli *Buddhavaṃsa*, as the personal name given by the brahman astrologers to the prince, but seems rarely to be used for the enlightened Buddha, except, perhaps, in modern books in English! A name for the Buddha used especially but not exclusively in Mahāyāna texts, is Śākyamuni, Sage of the Śākyas. The title was certainly in use by the time of the Emperor Aśoka in the third century BCE, found in the pillar edict in Lumbinī.

To make it entirely clear, the term *Buddha* is frequently qualified as the *completely perfected Buddha* (*samyak-saṃbuddha*), in contrast to the *pratyeka-buddha* mentioned above, who is enlightened yet does not systematically teach, and to *arhat*s, who have reached Enlightenment by following the path illuminated by a buddha. *Buddha* is not the only term used for the perfectly Enlightened. One term that was also much used from the time of the earliest texts, and also continues today, is the title *Tathāgata*, Thus-Gone or Thus-Come. The precise original meaning is not altogether clear but, like the term Buddha, in the early texts it is often used by the Buddha to refer to himself, especially when emphasising his special status. A similar term, *Sugata*, Gone-Happily (or perhaps more colloquially, Blissed-Out), is also found as an epithet in early texts, and continues to be used throughout Buddhist scriptures. Another term, *Jina* or Conqueror, is found less in the earliest Buddhist tradition but was used for the enlightened in the Jain tradition, and adopted in the Mahāyāna and tantric traditions, as an epithet for the Buddha or buddhas, one who conquers or vanquishes defilements or ignorance. The Buddha is also entitled the *Teacher* or the *Guide*. The Buddha may be Enlightened but few Buddhist schools see him as a saviour in the sense of one who can save a person who makes no effort. In most Buddhist traditions, the Buddha is the Guide who shows the way, but the person has to practise the spiritual path themselves. The analogy of the Buddha as a doctor or physician is also used: the Buddha diagnoses the problem with existence and prescribes the medicine, but the person has to take the medicine for the cure to work.

THE NATURE OF THE BUDDHA IN THE BUDDHIST TRADITION

THE BUDDHA: HUMAN, DIVINE, BOTH OR NEITHER?

The Buddha is considered pre-eminent in existence, but not a god. In early Buddhist texts, the Brahmanical gods honour and receive instruction from the Buddha. There is even a rather amusing incident in the Pāli *Mahāparinibbāna Sutta* mentioned above in which the Buddha advises an attendant to move aside, since he is blocking the view of large numbers of gods who are apparently crowding around the area to pay their last respects to the Buddha, unseen by the human disciples. That the gods are simply in a higher plane of existence but remain bound by the laws of cause and effect is not altogether different from some of the ancient Brahmanical assumptions about the Vedic ritual sacrifice, which the gods were bound to accept and reward if performed correctly by the ritual officiants. In Buddhism, however, the gods may be brought a little further down to earth. Accessibility to divine realms is seen as resulting from meditation training – and such results are by no means equated with the highest spiritual achievements. Birth as a god is seen as the result of meritorious or karmically fruitful deeds, but such a life is not eternal, even if it lasts so long as to *appear* eternal. In fact, the Pāli *Brahmajāla Sutta* of the *Dīgha Nikāya* (DN 1) pokes fun at the Brahmanical creator god Mahā-Brahmā, who may be the first to arise in a particular world system, through exhaustion of the merits through which he formerly resided in a more subtle divine abode, but then he deludedly assumes that he is creating the other creatures who appear after him.

The Buddha, then, is not a god, but he is certainly super-human in his spiritual status. To what extent might he be seen as a rather exceptional *human*? There may be a distinction here between the status of the bodhisattva still striving for liberation and the enlightened buddha. From the viewpoint of the early tradition, the bodhisattva shares the essentials of the human condition, still being subject to birth and death, yet, even in this case, by the time of the Buddha's final life, his previous life in a god realm, the exercise of choice over his birth and the miraculous manner of the birth, would seem to put him in a different category from human life in general. The tendency to see the bodhisattva both as unique and super-human becomes more marked in some later Buddhist traditions. Mahāyāna Buddhist approaches take further the technique of using the Buddha's life story as an allegorical demonstration of the spiritual path. From this perspective, the story is structured in this way not because it represents the history of a man striving for spiritual release, but because it represents an illustration of an ideal model of the spiritual path, a demonstration lived out by an already enlightened buddha for the sole purpose of inspiring students.

Whatever the status of the bodhisattva before his Enlightenment, the Buddhist tradition would seem to be united in seeing the enlightened Buddha as having surpassed the human condition. He is considered to have transcended the categories of ordinary beings, both those of humans and of gods and all other non-humans, attaining to a unique status. The Pāli *Dona Sutta* of the *Aṅguttara Nikāya* (AN 4.36) makes this explicit. In this text, the Buddha is questioned by an astonished brahmin who does not know what to make of the Buddha's appearance, asking him whether he is a god or another category of being, going in turn through the possibilities known in the ancient Indian context. To each alternative, including that of being a human, the Buddha replies, 'no'. Finally, when all suggestions have been exhausted, the Buddha explains that he is a Buddha, comparing himself to a beautiful lotus flower that has grown in the water, yet has risen above it. So, he is awakened, and untainted by the world. The Buddha's own declaration of a unique status recurs throughout the early scriptures, and was surely part of the earliest generation's truth claims for their master. It is less clear whether the earliest tradition claimed that the Buddha was omniscient, or whether there was some subtle distinction between the Enlightenment of the master and that attained subsequently by the students, although the overall impression is that the state of liberation was thought to be exactly the same. The disciples considered to have attained Enlightenment were referred to as *arhats* (Pāli *arahant*), not as buddhas, yet the Buddha is frequently also described as an arhat. Possible differences in the attainment of an arhat later became a topic for polemical dispute, but the main distinction in the early texts concerns rather the question of how Enlightenment was gained. The key difference is that it was the Buddha who made the initial discovery and who was indispensible as the perfect guide. The enlightened students continued to defer to him, for their own liberation had been dependent on his teaching. Moreover, the Buddha was considered to have additional knowledges and powers that were not necessarily accomplished by other arhats.

We have seen that the mythology which the tradition constructed around the figure of the Buddha emphasised the idea of the Buddha as a type rather than an individual, working out a long and carefully structured path of perfection over the ages, having continuity with previous buddhas and precise parallels with their trajectories. Each buddha uncovers the same truth about existence and how to gain release from it, a truth which has always existed but which is hard to find. The Buddha thus becomes a symbol of the Enlightened state or the transcendent goal. Some branches of the early Buddhist tradition, such as the Lokottaravāda order, put more emphasis on the transcendent nature of the Buddha than did the Theravāda tradition, and the later Mahāyāna developed this tendency further.

In a sense, Buddhist traditions all needed to find a balance in their doctrines between the transcendent and human aspects of the Buddha, and each school developed their own nuances. Christianity developed a doctrine of Christ as both fully human and divine, each aspect seeming to be equally necessary. Buddhism has no such dogma regarding the Buddha at its core, but Buddhist approaches may similarly emphasise both aspects of the Buddha's humanity and of his transcendence of human desires and misconceptions. That the Buddha had been human, and became enlightened from the human condition, demonstrates that it is possible for others to reach the same awakening. Even those forms of Buddhism that emphasise the transcendence of the Buddha throughout his final life, the idea that he was already enlightened, a mere manifestation of primordial buddhahood in some versions, still recognise the possibility of others following in his footsteps and attaining liberation from the world. In fact, the Mahāyāna traditions, which developed furthest theories of the Buddha as an eternal manifestation of enlightened wisdom, simultaneously stressed the validity of the bodhisattva path as an ideal and model for all to aspire for. The Buddha may be utterly transcendent, but the same state is attainable by others. In Buddhist scriptures of different traditions, Enlightenment is always presented as a possibility for other beings, even if in some cases a rather distant one, and the human state is especially presented as offering great potential for this ultimate spiritual goal.

On the other hand, Buddhist teachings would seem to make it necessary for the Buddha to be seen as a transcendent realised being, in some sense quite different from ordinary mortals. There is a fundamental doctrinal assumption of an opposition between the cycle of worldly existence and the Enlightenment or *nirvāṇa* which is attained by the Buddha. But this is not only a matter of doctrinal niceties. If the Buddha is merely human, how could he represent liberation and lead others to liberation from the wheel of conditioned existence? The importance of emphasising the Buddha's transcendence is connected practically with the efficacy of a spiritual path which, by its own admission, is seeking to undercut habitual tendencies rooted in everyday experience from lifetimes in the distant past. Developing trust or faith in the Buddha as embodying the Enlightened state, and expressing such faith in paying homage, is encouraged in the earliest texts. In the *Ariyapariyesana Sutta*, after his Enlightenment when about to begin teaching, the Buddha berates his five former companions for not showing the appropriate respect for one who is perfectly Enlightened. In the *Mahāsīhanāda* (Great Lion's Roar) *Sutta* in the Pāli *Majjhima Nikāya* (MN 12), the Buddha explains the *Ten Powers of a Tathāgata*, which are ten supernormal kinds of direct understanding relating to cause and effect, to the world and the faculties of beings, and to the three knowledges connected with Enlightenment (as explained above). The list continued to have its place in later Buddhism of different traditions.

MULTIPLE BUDDHAS

As will be clear from the above discussion, the Buddhist tradition soon developed the doctrine of different buddhas arising in different ages and in different world systems. Thus, the present Buddha of our world was considered to have trained under many previous buddhas during his long apprenticeship as a bodhisattva; the Theravāda names twenty-seven past buddhas. There is also mythology relating to the next Buddha, Maitreya (Pāli Metteyya), who is currently a bodhisattva residing in the Tusita heaven. A prophecy concerning him is given in the *Cakkavatti-Sīhanāda* (Wheel-turning Lion's Roar) *Sutta* in the Pāli *Dīgha Nikāya* (DN 26), and more detailed stories grew up in time, such as the Sanskrit *Lalitavistara* hagiography of the Buddha, which has the bodhisattva handing on his tiara to Maitreya when he leaves the Tusita to descend to earth. At various times, Maitreya cults have been associated with Millenarian movements, but more typically his reign is considered rather far off in the future.

In the Mahāyāna tradition, the notion of different buddhas in different world systems and eras was developed in a way that allowed for the possibility of multiple buddhas arising simultaneously. The idea is connected with various aspects of Mahāyāna doctrine, developed in a re-working of Buddhist teaching classified as a second *Turning of the Dharma Wheel* (see above on the first *Turning*). In the early teachings, whether or not a Tathāgata exists after his parinirvāṇa was one of the ultimate questions which the Buddha did not answer, on the grounds that they were wrongly formulated or distract students from the important matter of getting enlightened (e.g., the *Aggi-vacchagotta Sutta* in the Pāli *Majjhima Nikāya* MN 72). But the hints that even if the usual categories of existence and non-existence do not apply, the Tathāgata's state is deep, immeasurable and unfathomable, are enough to suggest some kind of existence. The Mahāyāna teaching took shape that the demonstration of the final nirvāṇa was purely a skilful technique to emphasise the teaching of impermanence and discourage complacency, but that really the Buddha lives on for aeons or even eternally, and is accessible. Moreover, the great powers of buddhas make it possible for the buddhas of other world systems to communicate across vast distances. This is also graphically illustrated in Mahāyāna sūtras by visits from buddhas of the past who were supposed to have entered extinction long ago, or visions of buddhas residing in other worlds, brought into communication through the Buddha's inspiration.

The Mahāyāna movement's new scriptural revelations included some sūtras focused on other such buddhas from distant world systems. Two around whom cults grew up were the Buddha Amitābha and the Medicine Buddha, the Tathāgata of Azure Radiance. Both had their own sūtras, featuring the list of vows made when they were bodhisattvas. Amitābha's vows include the promise to help any beings who call out to him to be reborn in his pure Buddha field, Sukhāvatī, while the Medicine Buddha promises especially to help liberate the sick and the weak. Amitābha (= Amida in Japan) became particularly popular in East Asian Buddhism, the Pure Land Buddhist schools focused exclusively on him. The sūtras and practices associated with him also had long-lasting impact on Northern Buddhism, not as a separate cult but in the genre of prayers for rebirth in his Buddha field, and in tantric practices focused on ejecting the consciousness to his Buddha field at the time of death. The Medicine Buddha cult also spread throughout Mahāyāna areas, both East Asian and Northern. In Tibet, meditation on the Medicine Buddha was integrated into the traditional medical training.

Tantric Buddhism added further Buddhas, not always conceptualised as former bodhisattvas perfecting particular accomplishments, but often more explicitly explained as embodiments of primordial Enlightenment, manifesting enlightened qualities of different types which can be transmitted and perfected through tantric initiation and practice. The tantric cult of the Buddha Vairocana has been especially significant in East Asian tantric traditions, and also of importance historically in the first wave of Buddhist transmission in Tibet in the eighth and ninth centuries CE. A plethora of Buddhas and tantric deities are found in Northern Buddhism, which built on the already vast Buddhist tantric literature and traditions imported to Tibet from Pāla dynasty Bengal. Historically, tantric Buddhism also influenced South-east Asian cultures.

BUDDHA BODIES

Different kinds of buddha manifestations are related to doctrines concerning buddha bodies, especially the late Mahāyāna triple body doctrine. An early distinction had been made between the Buddha's body of material form (*rūpakāya*) and his Dharma body (*dharmakāya*). The distinction arose out of statements attributed to the Buddha in the early texts, in which he suggests an identification between himself and his Dharma. For instance, in the *Vakkali Sutta* of the *Samyutta Nikāya* (SN 22.87), when his student Vakkali is expressing sadness at having been ill and thus unable to see the Buddha personally, the Buddha responds by asking what there is to see in his impure physical body, adding that whoever sees the Dhamma, sees the Buddha. In the *Digha Nikāya's Aggañña Sutta* (DN 27), the Buddha states that the Tathāgata is designated as one who has a *Dhamma body*. Such statements can be taken in a straightforward manner simply to mean that the Buddha is to be defined by the corpus of his teaching, but the term implies the discovered truth as well as the teachings about it. In later Mahāyāna interpretation, the *dharmakāya* comes to mean the ultimate truth 'body' of the Buddha, the unconditioned enlightened state beyond any physical manifestation. In time, the *rūpakāya* was further analysed into two aspects. First, there is the perfected body of enjoyment, or *sambhogakāya*, radiant and pure buddha forms of enlightened qualities existing in pure buddha fields, and generally perceptible only to the advanced bodhisattvas in their retinues. Second, there is the emanated body, the *nirmāṇakāya*, which is the manifested physical forms of the Buddha in the world.

In tantric practice, the *dharmakāya* is the enlightened buddha mind, the purified nature of conscious thinking, the *sambhogakāya* is buddha speech, the expressive and communicative qualities of Enlightenment vibrating within sounds, while the *nirmāṇakāya* is buddha body, actually appearing enlightened manifestations.

THE BUDDHA WITHIN AND WITHOUT

Mahāyāna and tantric ideas and practices connected with multiple buddhas and buddha manifestations spring principally from various visionary *sūtra*s and, later, texts called *tantra*s, which emphasised the idea of transforming one's view, thus relating to the enlightened nature within the conditioned world. In the opening chapter of the early Mahāyāna *Vimalakīrtinirdeśasūtra*, the Elder monk, Śāriputra, is lectured on failing to see the pure nature of our world because of the precipices and chasms in his mind, and the Buddha proceeds to demonstrate the real condition of his pure buddha field – which is our world – by touching the land with his toe, whereupon the world is revealed as an enlightened display of dazzling jewels. The *Vimalakīrtinirdeśa* also hints at a doctrine of interpenetrating worlds, when at the Buddha's instigation, Vimalakīrti uses his psychic power to grasp the Abhirati buddha field of the Tathāgata Akṣobhya in his right hand to show the assembly, but although the buddha field is reduced to practically nothing by this feat, it still remains the same size, and equally, our world is neither augmented nor diminished. A rather amusing subplot is that the Abhirati residents who have achieved the divine eye become perturbed at being carried off and complain to Akṣobhya, who declines to intervene, but those gods and humans who have yet to reach this level notice nothing and remain calm.

In the rather later *Avataṃsakasūtra*, which had a major impact on East Asian Buddhism, not only the school which focused on it (*Huayan*, Japanese *Kegon*) but also the *Chan* (= Japanese *Zen*) school, we find the vision of innumerable buddhas residing in a single atom, filling every universe, yet remaining intact within their own vast buddha fields, and aeons penetrated in a single moment, so that the buddhas of past, present and future are simultaneously perceived. Extracts from the *Avataṃsaka* literature and similarly worded liturgies of Aspirations are used throughout Tibetan Buddhist traditions, and this kind of perspective appears to be embedded within many of the Northern Buddhist tantric practices, focusing on transforming oneself, the world and its inhabitants into the enlightened manifestations of buddhas and buddha fields. In this way, ordinary body, speech and mind is experienced as the Buddha's *nirmāṇakāya*, *sambhogakāya* and *dharmakāya*, respectively. Short of such meditative achievement, there is also the idea that given an auspicious connection with the Buddha's teaching, as the path unfolds, there may be omens and signs indicating the Buddha's, Guru's or enlightened deity's presence, in some sense manifestations of the *nirmāṇakāya* in the everyday world. Nonetheless, the contrast between ordinary unenlightened experience and the buddha reality holds good and provides the incentive for spiritual practice. The incomplete *nirmāṇakāya* of any ordinary being or object which inspires a sense of the Buddha's presence is to be distinguished from the *completely perfected nirmāṇakāya* of a fully enlightened buddha.

Finally, it is worth mentioning the later Mahāyāna *Buddha Nature* doctrine, which is sometimes linked to the third *Turning of the Dharma Wheel*. This teaching seeks to comment on the possibility of transformation from an unenlightened being into a buddha by showing that ordinary beings share the same *buddha nature*, which simply needs to be developed or revealed. In some versions, the *buddha nature*, called the *tathāgatagarbha* in Sanskrit, the *Embryo of the Tathāgata*, or the *Sugata Essence* (*bde gshegs snying po*) in Tibetan, is compared to an inner seed which needs to be nurtured so that it will grow and finally flower as a buddha. Natural goodness and virtue, compassion and the inclination for spiritual growth, all demonstrate the *Embryo of the Tathāgata*, without which no Buddhist practice could bear fruit. Some versions of the teaching assumed that the most evil beings are hopeless cases, lacking the *Embryo of the Tathāgata*, but the versions of the doctrine with the most long-term success stressed that every single being shares it, even if it may be covered in layer upon layer of defilement, which needs to be removed for them finally to attain buddhahood. Other presentations of the doctrine, which were especially influential in traditions such as East Asian Chan/Zen and Northern tantric teachings, emphasised the idea that the *buddha nature* may be seen not so much as a seed which must be nourished and grow, but rather as a fully developed naturally enlightened state. According to this view, this already perfected condition has simply been obscured and needs only to be uncovered for Enlightenment to manifest, rather like the sun emerging spontaneously from behind the clouds.

VENERATION OF THE BUDDHA

If – as all Buddhists would hold – the Buddha is perfectly enlightened and lacks nothing; if – as in the early and still in the Theravāda tradition – the Buddha has passed into the final Nirvāna and is inaccessible; if – as in some Mahāyāna and tantric perspectives – we are all really buddhas or have the buddha within, then what purpose could be served in bowing, chanting to, or making offerings to the Buddha? There are two levels on which this question can be answered, but first it should be said that virtually all traditional Buddhist schools do encourage such forms of veneration, and it would seem to have been part of the earliest Buddhist teaching. On the one hand, from what might be called the doctrinal level, ritual worship can be seen as expressing and developing faith and commitment, as creating virtuous thoughts which will translate into good karma which can stay with the worshipper from one lifetime to the next, and as generating application and receptivity to the mental factors useful for spiritual progress. Thus, there is a popular Tibetan practice in which a mirror held before a buddha image is washed, to the accompaniment of verses of recitation noting that the Buddha is perfect and has no need of the offering, yet our own clouded view needs to be purified. Secondly, from what might be called the symbolic level, ritual worship is not so much a means–ends-orientated activity, but has an important expressive dimension. To use Wittgenstein's example of kissing the picture or name of a loved one, which we hardly imagine will affect the lover, rituals may be performed for our own expressive needs. Thus, venerating the Buddha may have its own rationale and effect on the person, which may have little or nothing to do with the extent to which they may or may not understand the doctrine about the Buddha.

As mentioned above, showing deference and respect to the Buddha, making pilgrimage to the sites associated with the Buddha, and constructing and worshipping stūpas containing the Buddha's relics, were early forms of Buddhist worship. The chance to give alms to the Buddha was also considered a precious privilege during the Buddha's lifetime. Clockwise circumambulation of the Buddha or a stūpa or pilgrimage site, keeping the right shoulder towards the object of veneration was another ancient practice that has continued up until today. What changed most was the objects that were the focus of worship. The Buddhist stūpa began as what was originally an ancient Indian burial mound or rounded tomb, apparently erected to hold the Buddha's ashes. The form and structure developed, in part connected with an internal Buddhist reflection on the imagery for representing Enlightenment, so that different aspects of Buddhist understanding or the path to realisation could be symbolically depicted, and, in part, the changing stūpa forms illustrate different styles of architecture in different areas. The earliest stūpas are large domes, or cylinder-shaped constructions rounded at the top. Later stūpas became rather slimmer, often tapering up to pointed tops, and also evolved into multi-roofed pagodas, as in China and Japan. Tibetan stūpas are often very elaborate in design, each part full of religious symbolism, and representative of different enlightened qualities and aspects of the enlightened person. Stūpas came to contain relics other than bodily remains, including texts, buddha images and other sacred items, and small votive stūpas could also be made to place on a shrine or as an offering in a holy place.

But the most remarkable innovation was the use of buddha images, beginning only in the early centuries CE in the areas of Gandhāra, situated in what is now northern Pakistan and eastern Afghanistan, and Mathura, in northern India, now within the area of Uttar Pradesh. Devotional practices (*bhakti*) were developing in other Indian religions in this era, although it would be a mistake to believe that Buddhists had not venerated the Buddha before they had images. It seems rather that the early attitude was that lesser beings could be represented validly in such imagery, but that the Buddha was too eminent for such coarse treatment, so he was represented by the stūpa or other symbolic forms. Nonetheless, the development marks a rather new kind of packaging of religious practice, even a new kind of sacred building, as simple assembly halls for monks were gradually replaced by temples housing buddha images. Some of the early forms of buddha images show the influence of Greek and Central Asian traditions of imagery. As in the case of stūpas and other Buddhist imagery, the particular forms again reflect regional cultural styles, as well as embodying the Buddhist symbolism. A statue or a painting may be used. The Buddha is often depicted in a serene meditative pose, or making gestures symbolising, for instance, the giving of teaching or the attainment of Enlightenment. As well as representing the Buddha himself, a Buddha image expresses the enlightened state, and reminds the person that perfection can be attained as a human.

Pictures and statues for worship are also made of other Buddhist saints, such as the Buddha's disciples and early saints (the arhats), and bodhisattva figures in Mahāyāna contexts. Buddha images are made not only of the historical Buddha but also of other buddhas considered to be the enlightened ones of different times and world systems, and such imagery becomes central in some Mahāyāna traditions, as we have seen above.

In tantric traditions, images and paintings are also made of other 'deity' figures, representing particular aspects of enlightened qualities which are meditated upon and identified with, to develop the same qualities within one's own mind. In the case of depictions of fierce deities, the imagery may be intended to transform the energies of aggression into their enlightened nature, which may be conceived of, say, as destroying the emotional defilements or the forces of ignorance personified as Māra and his hordes.

The main purpose of images and painting of buddha figures, then, is for devotional worship and meditative contemplation. There are consecration rituals that are considered to transform the object so that it can really embody the presence of the Buddha. Consecrations in a Southern Buddhist context may begin with the new image being charged with qualities by connecting it to an old established image via a circle of sacred thread passed along a line of monks and encircling the new image. Some monks may sit silently while others chant and transfer virtues. The more accomplished the monks are as meditators, the more effective this process is considered to be. The culminating rite is that of 'opening the eyes' of the image, through removal of a cloth covering and sometimes cleansing the eyes with oil. Once such a ceremony has been performed, it is important for the image to be treated with respect and devotion.

On the one hand, there is the idea that the image can support one's religious practice, so in making prostrations, offerings, or contemplating the Buddha's qualities, this will have a direct impact on the mind and will help to generate virtue which will bring good karmic results. But there is also a sense in which consecrated images are often considered to take on a power of their own, and to radiate blessings upon their environment. This is especially the case if they contain relics or have some association with a great master of the past, or if they have been consecrated by a famous meditation teacher, or have a special history or value.

CHAPTER SUMMARY

- Academic histories of the Buddha necessarily rely a good deal on later Buddhist sources which often structure the material to highlight Buddhist doctrines rather than fact.
- We can nonetheless distinguish between early and later traditions about the Buddha.
- The Buddha drew on the heritage of Brahmanical culture, and also the sub-culture of renouncer hermits, from which he emerged.
- Even early traditions of the Buddha's life included mythological elements.
- The earliest accounts focus on the Buddha's experience as an adult renouncer and his Enlightenment, seeking to relate them to the Buddha's teaching.
- The later accounts integrate the stories into more elaborate hagiographies based around the Buddha's Acts.
- The Buddha is considered to have a unique status, neither exactly divine nor human.
- Early teachings on various buddhas in different ages of the world developed into Mahāyāna teachings on multiple buddhas.
- Further doctrines on buddha bodies, buddha manifestations, and the buddha within are also found in Mahāyāna and tantric traditions.
- The worship of buddhas, through the stūpa cult and through buddha images, spans the whole of Asian Buddhism.

FURTHER READING

ON THE LIFE OF THE BUDDHA

Carrithers, Michael 1983 *The Buddha*. A short study focusing only on early sources.

Mahidol University, Bangkok. 2002 *An Illustrated Life of the Buddha* www. budsir.org/MenuEng.htm A traditional Thai Theravāda presentation of the Buddha's life story, with illustrations.

Pye, Michael 1979 *The Buddha*. A useful source, seeking to separate out history, early traditions, and the later hagiographic accounts.

Snellgrove, David L 1987 *Indo-Tibetan Buddhism: Indian Buddhists and their Tibetan successors*. I. Section 2–4 on the Buddha and buddhahood; II. Section 2 on Buddha images and multiple buddhas.

Strong, John 2001 *The Buddha, A Short Biography*. An exploration of the stories and imagery surrounding the Buddha.

Tambiah, Stanley 1984 *The Buddhist Saints of the Forest and the Cult of Amulets: A Study in Charisma, Hagiography, Sectarianism and Millennial Buddhism*. See pages 230–57 for description of the consecration of buddha images.

SCRIPTURAL SOURCES ON THE BUDDHA'S LIFE

Bullitt, John 2009 *Access to Insight: Readings in Theravada Buddhism* www. accesstoinsight.org/ English translations of many Pāli texts by various scholars, with an index of *sutta* (discourse) names.

Conze, Edward 1959 *Buddhist Scriptures*. Part I on the Buddha, includes a long but condensed series of extracts from Aśvaghoṣa's *Buddhacarita*.

Nārada Mahā Thera 1973 *The Buddha and His Teachings*. An account of the Buddha, consisting mostly of short Pāli scriptural citations.

Walshe, Maurice 1995 *The Long Discourses of the Buddha: A Translation of the Dīgha Nikāya*. Full translation, also including useful notes on interesting or questionable readings.

The Tipitaka www.metta.lk/tipitaka/ A Sri Lankan website on the Pāli Canon. For many texts, the Pali and Sinhala versions are available; in some sections there are also English translations of large parts.

MAHĀYĀNA SŪTRAS

Cleary, Thomas (Translated from Chinese) 1987 *The Flower Ornament Scripture. The Avatamsaka Sutra*. See especially the final pages of Volume 3, the Samantabhadra (Universally Good) Aspiration, pp. 387–94.

Lamotte, Étienne 1976 *The Teaching of Vimalakīrti (Vimalakīrtinirdeśa)*. Translated by S. Boin. Very scholarly translation and study of the *Vimalakī- rtinirdeśasūtra*, with reference to more than one edition, and variant readings included.

THE DHARMA

THE MEANING OF DHARMA

In Hindu traditions, the term *dharma* suggests one's duty and way of life, especially the duties associated with one's caste status. These duties may be considered divinely ordained, and connected to a natural law of how things should be, so that *dharma* also indicates a righteous order throughout the cosmos. Thus, the gods of Hindu mythology seek to maintain order or *dharma*, while the anti-gods threaten this order, although ultimately repeatedly fail to upset it. Buddhism re-interpreted the concept for the Jewel of the *Buddha-Dharma*. One aspect of the *Dharma's* significance is that it is the truth of how things are, but instead of indicating a cosmic order which should be maintained by religious practice, it indicates the patterns of conditioned existence, the understanding of how to transcend that unhappy order, and the realisation achieved as a result. The *Dharma* is thus the Buddhist teachings, the spiritual path and the truths indicated by that path. Another Buddhist meaning of the word *dharma*, which is quite distinct from the connotations of the Dharma Jewel of the Buddha's teachings, is that of the many elemental basic processes of existence, the real but ever-changing components underlying the compounded realities which we experience. Books in English have established a convention of using a small letter 'd' for talking about such *dharma*s. The classification and analysis of these *dharma*s and what kind of reality they may or may not have became an important part of Buddhist philosophy, which we will introduce briefly below.

The *Dharma* is the second sacred Jewel in Buddhism to which adherents go for Refuge. As we have seen above, the *Dharma-body* may be equated with the Buddha, and, in Mahāyāna, the Dharma-body of the Buddha (*dharmakāya*) comes to indicate the ultimate Enlightened state. But in the sense of the *spiritual path*, the Dharma is considered necessary as a vehicle and to uphold the spiritual practitioner, but not always equated with the final goal. Thus, an early analogy was the Dharma as a raft (e.g., in the *Majjhima Nikāya*'s *Alagaddūpama Sutta* MN 22), allowing the spiritual practitioner to cross from the near shore of existence and reach the other shore of Enlightenment (*nirvāṇa*). When the other shore is arrived at, the raft of the Dharma can be put aside.

THE DHARMA AS A SPIRITUAL PATH: THE SINGLE TRUE REALITY AND WAY, OR THE MANY ROUTES

Often, Buddhism seems to represent two almost contradictory approaches, which each Buddhist tradition strives to reconcile in its own way. On the one hand, Buddhism tends to have a universalistic approach to ethics and to spiritual growth. Buddhism rejected the particularism of Brahmanism, which considered some actions appropriate and morally correct for one hereditary group, while being inappropriate and wrong for another. From the Buddhist viewpoint, taking life, for instance, is morally wrong, and saving life is morally good for everyone. Moreover, there is the assumption that not only all humans, but also other living beings are fundamentally similar in their basic psychology, such as wanting to be happy and to avoid suffering. And the analysis embodied in Buddhist teachings assumes a universal applicability. We all have the same existential problems, and the removal of the factors considered to be the causes of these problems is emphasised to be necessary for everyone's spiritual progress. Moreover, as it is put in the Pāli *Uposatha Sutta* in the *Udāna* collection of the *Khuddaka Nikāya* (Ud 5.5), the Dharma is said to have a single taste, like the salty taste throughout a great ocean, it has everywhere the same flavour of liberation.

At the same time, there is also the idea that there can be many different routes; the Dharma raft may come in rather different shapes and sizes, many different routes may carry the raft across the river to the 'other shore'. Often, the round figure of '84,000' Dharmas or teachings are referred to. There was a Tibetan saying that every lama has his own practice, as every district has its own dialect (*bla ma re la phyag len re/ lung pa re la skad lugs re*). In the earliest texts, there is considerable variation. The Buddha had a long teaching career, perhaps from age thirty-five to eighty if the traditional accounts are correct. The early texts present the Buddha as responding to the opinions and experiences of his audiences, so teachings to monks, to brahmins, to kings, to traders, to farmers, etc. may be rather different in content. But this is not all. There are also some rather different suggestions given to monastics about the ways to attain Enlightenment. It is possible that the Buddha himself developed his presentation over the years, and it is also possible that different emphases we find in the early texts represented different approaches amongst the early students. In Mahāyāna Buddhism, to embrace rather different methods comes to be seen technically as '*skilful means*', a doctrine suggesting that different techniques may be useful in bringing spiritual development. This is not simply a matter of developing alternative ways to say or to effect the same thing. It may go a good deal further than that, in the idea that it is possible to present teachings which at first sight would appear to have quite different objectives from the 'single taste of liberation' and yet may lead the individual onto the spiritual path which ultimately will take them to the same goal. The Buddhist assumption that an individual's spiritual development may take place over innumerable lifetimes also engenders a rather ecumenical approach. A belief or practice which may have limitations at an advanced level may nonetheless be useful at an early stage, so it could be harmful to the person's spiritual progress to interfere or criticise.

THE STORY OF NANDA

Generally, the *skilful means* doctrine is associated with Mahāyāna Buddhism, but there is a striking example in the early texts which shows that the principles were well established quite early on. Nanda was the Buddha's younger cousin and half-brother. The *Nanda Sutta* story goes that young Nanda was enamoured of a young woman when he took monastic ordination. In the more embellished version of the story, it was the Buddha who told him to become a monk as he was about to marry, and the unfortunate Nanda felt obligated to consent since the Buddha was a senior kinsman. In any event, the *Nanda Sutta* makes it clear that Nanda was miserable as a monk. He made no progress whatsoever in his spiritual endeavour, since he could only think about the lovely girl he had lost. Eventually, he confessed this to the Buddha, who then took him on a visit to a heavenly world, where he saw the most wonderful divine nymphs who entirely dispelled any thought of the young woman's charms. The Buddha guaranteed that he could have five hundred such nymphs so long as he lived the holy life under the Buddha's guidance, perhaps by perfecting the deep absorptions which have divine rebirth as a side effect. Nanda therefore devoted himself to this training. However, other monks who heard the story, possibly jealous of the attentions Nanda had received from the Buddha or of his visit to a heaven, started to gossip about Nanda doing religious practice in order to get five hundred nymphs. Nanda was teased and ridiculed so badly that he eventually generated real renunciation for worldly goals, went into solitary retreat, and was able to apply himself to the goal of Enlightenment, which he swiftly achieved.

(The *Nanda Sutta* is in the Pāli *Udāna* collection of the *Khuddaka Nikāya* Ud 3.2.)

DISTINGUISHING THE DHARMA FROM NON-DHARMA

If the Dharma can appear in different formulations, the question arises how an authentic Dharma teaching may be recognised. The early texts give a number of answers to this question, and these answers continue to be referred to in later times. The most significant points, which are not altogether consistent, can be summarised as follows:

(1) Reliance should *not* be placed solely on the teacher's account of having received the teaching from the Buddha or another

authentic teacher. Even if the account is not false, the teaching might have been misinterpreted. Nor should one rely on the teaching because it is given by one's own teacher, nor because the teacher seems powerful, or because it fits with tradition.

(2) The teaching should be investigated carefully and one should reach one's own conclusions, *not* with reference to one's own preferences or ideas, nor through logical reasoning nor pondering probabilities, but through the following procedures.

(3) Having examined the teaching's wording and expression, it should be compared with the teachings established in the collection of the Buddha's discourses and the texts on monastic discipline, and, if it is in line with them, then it can be trusted.

(4) The teaching can be trusted if it develops qualities which, 'lead to dispassion, not to passion; to being unfettered, not to being fettered; to shedding, not to accumulating; to modesty, not to self-aggrandizement; to contentment, not to discontent; to seclusion, not to entanglement; to aroused persistence, not to laziness; to being unburdensome, not to being burdensome' (*Gotami Sutta* AN 8.53).

It will be seen readily that either points (3) and (4) could follow on from points (1) and (2), but (3) and (4) are quite different arguments. The third point is found (amongst other places) in the *Dīgha Nikāya*'s *Mahāparinibbāna Sutta* (DN 16), where what was at issue was the Dharma's continuity when the Buddha was about to pass away. In some ways, it is quite open; it is not restricting the Dharma only to what has already been said. However, especially in the context where the Buddha's representatives had to make decisions about what was to be allowed into the corpus of scriptures and what was to be excluded, the point would seem to tend towards conservatism. The fourth point, as phrased above, from the *Gotami Sutta* of the *Aṅguttara Nikāya* (although again found elsewhere with variant nuances), would seem much more open to new formulations. Here, the context is that of an individual practitioner about to enter secluded retreat, and needing a way to check that her understanding of the Dharma was correct. Hence, the inner investigation is emphasised, and the impact of the teaching on the person. The claim that what characterises the Buddha Dharma is that it leads away from suffering and leads to liberation from suffering and to Enlightenment is oft repeated in Buddhist texts of all ages. While it implies an openness to variants in presentation, it also implies a fairly unified perspective on the contrast between suffering and the round of conditioned existence (*saṃsāra*) on the one hand and liberation and *nirvāṇa* on the other.

It is also worth noting that point (1) continued to have some force in both the contexts of establishing the textual heritage and in meditative training, but respect for one's teacher and reliance on an authentic lineage of transmission also became central principles. In fact, this was doubtless the case from the start, which is perhaps why there is such an emphasis on the point that trust in the teacher should not be considered sufficient for certainty when there is any question over the teaching's authenticity.

THE FOUR TRUTHS OF THE NOBLE ONES

The Four Truths are a very influential presentation of the central Buddhist teachings, and traditionally equated with the Buddha's first teaching or *Turning of the Dharma Wheel* at Sarnath. Books in English generally speak of the 'Four Noble Truths', but many Asian Buddhists have objected to the shorthand not simply on the grounds that it is inappropriate grammatically, but more seriously because the first and second Truths cannot be described as 'noble'. In Asian languages, the term 'noble' refers to those who are noble, that is, the Buddha and/or other advanced spiritual beings who are irreversibly on the path to Enlightenment, and the path itself. Thus, the Truths are the truth as seen by, or Truths *for* the Noble Ones. In fact, the Truths embodied in the fourfold formulation are also taught in the context of many other Buddhist teachings, both early and late, and in different traditions. Here, the discussion of the Truths is not confined purely to teachings given within the Four Truth framework.

THE TRUTH OF SUFFERING

The first Truth is that life is characterised by *suffering* or *duḥkha*. The presentation as given in the *Dhammacakkappavattana Sutta* (SN 56.11) specifically includes birth, ageing, sickness and death, pain, sadness, failing to attain what one wants and instead encountering what is undesirable. All these are very familiar to the human condition. In some modern English discussions of the first Truth, it may be suggested that the Truth teaches about *human* suffering, but in fact it is far broader than this. It applies to all living beings and, indeed, in Buddhist philosophical analysis, it is applied to the whole of conditioned existence.

In Buddhist teaching, it is emphasised that nowhere is exempt from suffering: even the heavenly worlds are impermanent and, although the gods have very long lifetimes which may seem eternal, this makes the shock and suffering greater when their lives draw to a close and they perceive that they are likely to be born in a less happy state. Buddhism inherited Indian categories of different beings but integrated them into a neat set exemplifying different possible conditions of rebirth in the wheel of existence. Thus, the gods are inclined to be proud, complacent, and perhaps self-indulgent in the case of lesser gods. The powerful anti-gods of Hindu mythology who make war upon the gods become, in Buddhism, jealous gods, suffering through their continual fruitless striving to wrest power from the gods. Together with humans, these are the higher planes of rebirth. The three lower realms in which suffering is greater and more persistent are considered to have far larger populations. Animals are considered to be more at the mercy of their instincts than humans and less able to free themselves from miserable conditions in which they may be predator or prey, or subjected to abuse from humans. *Preta* spirits or ghosts may seek out offerings dedicated to them, but they can gain no satisfaction from the normal foods they attempt to eat. Despite their hunger, greed and their huge stomachs, they are considered to have very narrow necks which prevent them ever being full and satisfied. The vast numbers and sub-categories of denizens of hell drive home the point that the overall tendency within the wheel is to slip downwards. The hell beings are consumed in a world of aggression, torture and horror. But like the gods, their lives are far longer than humans, so their torments seem eternal.

Modern presentations of the different realms sometimes treat them as psychological conditions which may all be experienced by humans. Thus, the god realms indicate a state of luxury, pride and complacency, the jealous gods symbolise competitive striving for power and influence, the hell realms are states of deep despair and aggression, and so forth. Clearly, in a world in which belief in rebirth may not be a common shared assumption, such an interpretation may be a way of practising Buddhism without making a commitment to Buddhist beliefs which cannot be proven. The approach also builds on an important aspect of the traditional teachings, which had already taken up mythological categories and integrated them in a way which made them symbolic of Buddhist-defined psychological states with ethical overtones. Thus, we already find explicit associations between the emotional affliction of hatred and the hell realms, greed or desire and the *preta* spirits, delusion and animals, pride and gods, jealousy and the anti-gods, with the human condition considered to indicate a mix of all the afflictions. So rebirth in the three lower realms is to be avoided by avoidance of the most negative afflictions of hatred, greed or desire, and delusion. But in the traditional teachings, there is no doubt that the realms are seen as real states of existence into which one can actually be reborn and, at this time, most Buddhists continue to accept this perspective.

In traditional teachings on the first Truth, suffering is classified into three kinds:

- The suffering of suffering. This refers to obvious suffering, that which is painful, and is considered the predominant condition in the lower realms, as well as occurring more intermittently in the human world.
- The suffering of change. This may be sadness at the loss of a happy condition, or at the development of an unhappy condition. Ultimately, even if we are blessed with consistently happy lives, there is no escaping death. The suffering of change may also refer to rather more subtle suffering as a result of the fact of change, such as an underlying sense of sadness or unease even at the happiest moments, since one is aware of impermanence, and perhaps trying to cling on and avoid change. Or there may be a sense that one cannot relax and enjoy pleasant situations, since there is constant movement and flux.
- The pervasive suffering of conditioned existence. This is the most subtle level, referring to insidious frustrations or a state of unease or unrest at the heart of conditioned phenomena. In this sense, a translation of *duḥkha* as 'suffering', or when the word is

used in an adjectival sense, as 'painful', is a little inadequate, although it works perfectly well for the other categories. The *Dhammacakkappavattana Sutta* list ends by saying that in short, the five aggregates – form, feeling, perception, volitional activities, consciousness – are *duḥkha*. Sometimes, it is commented on quite simply with reference to chains of cause and effect. For instance, the nineteenth-century Tibetan master, Patrul Rinpoche, explained that it can refer to suffering which may be a necessary concomitant to happy conditions we experience. For example, to savour a cup of tea may seem an entirely innocent pleasure. However, Patrul Rinpoche points out in a line of reasoning which would seem to prefigure contemporary Green thinking on global economics, the cup of tea has necessitated the deaths of small creatures during the planting and harvesting of the tea in China, the suffering of the porters who carried it to the Tibetan border town, the suffering of the yaks and mules who were forced to transport the tea further into Tibet on their backs, as well as the cheating of merchants who traded it en route, and, through these exchanges, involvement with the production and sale of animal products. In Buddhist thinking on causation, one may also store up the prospects of future suffering as a result of enjoying happiness now at the expense of others.

On one level, the fact of suffering may seem so obvious in life that it is hard to see why it should be a Truth of Noble Ones – surely, every living being is aware of suffering? One point here is that suffering may be obscured or ignored, rather as one's own mortality may be forgotten or put to the back of the mind, and this avoidance may impede spiritual growth from a Buddhist perspective. A second point is that even when the experience of suffering is recognised, its nature may not be. One definition of ignorance in Buddhism includes the idea of relating to what is in fact suffering as though it were desirable and satisfactory. Apparently attractive delightful conditions may in fact bring suffering to ourselves and others, so, in Buddhist terms, they would be pain inducing and thus unidentified *duḥkha*.

Occasionally in discussions in English sources, Buddhist analysis of suffering may almost be reduced to consideration of impermanence, that is, the second aspect of suffering. This is clearly important in

Buddhist thinking, but ideas about moral causation are also central. In particular, there is the belief that in the unskilful pursuit of happiness, the future causes of suffering are in reality created. Serious immoral or unskilful acts such as taking life may bring short-term satisfaction but, according to Buddhist thinking, will result in shortened painful lives in the future, and both the hardening of habit patterns of violent behaviour and angry states, and the invitation of violence towards oneself.

THE TRUTH OF THE CAUSE OF SUFFERING

The second Truth identifies the root cause of suffering as craving, literally, thirst (*tṛṣṇā*). It is craving for satisfaction, happiness, success, material acquisition, and for the avoidance of unpleasant conditions, poverty, loss, blame, and so forth, which is considered responsible for suffering, both through the direct frustration of grasping unsuccessfully for desirable states and through the bad karma and hence longer-term suffering brought by achievement of one's own happiness at the cost of the happiness of others. This does not mean that all desires are considered unhelpful or evil in Buddhist thinking: commentaries elaborate that craving can be defined as the desire for pleasure, for existence and for non-existence. The desire for liberation is seen as positive and to be cultivated, as are selfless wishes to help others.

Some formulations of the second Truth add a qualification: the root problem is craving or desire, impelled by ignorance (*avidyā*). One gives into craving because one is unable to see its problematic implications. In particular, there is a failure to perceive directly and to understand the three signs or marks of conditioned existence: suffering, impermanence, and the lack of any self-nature. Thus, an early definition of ignorance in Buddhist doctrine is to view what is suffering related as though it were satisfactory, to see the impermanent as though it were permanent, that which lacks any self-nature as though it had such self-nature, and to view what is repulsive (involving indulgence in the most negative afflictions) as though it were delightful.

At the same time, we are dealing here with a circular situation: the ignorant view is conditioned by the emotional craving which prevents clear perception. The early texts include a few slightly different versions of a summarised analysis of the causal processes of conditioned existence in terms of a number of dependent links. These became standardised into a classic list of twelve links of dependent arising, with each factor giving rise to the next, and the process recurring, creating a continuous circle. Ignorance is the first of the links and craving is the eighth. The chain can be broken at either of the two places. In some Buddhist teachings, the problem of craving or desire is emphasised, while others focus more on ignorance. It is hard to generalise about different usages because different balances may be in evidence within the same school, as they were in the various presentations amongst the early texts. However, it is often in meditation teachings that the need to develop mental peace in calming down craving comes to the fore-front. The problem of ignorance, on the other hand, is more likely to dominate the more intellectual methods of developing wisdom. We shall have more to say later about the dual Buddhist interest in meditation and in scholarship, and the occasional evidence of tension between meditators and scholars. However, contrasts in emphasis should not be overstated, especially since meditators are also seeking to develop insight and wisdom, even if using less intellectual techniques than scholars.

THE TRUTH OF THE CESSATION OF SUFFERING

The third Truth continues the sequence with the next logical step: suffering can be extinguished through the removal of the cause, that is, through the stopping of craving. Thirty years ago, it was not uncommon for academic classes on Buddhism to discuss whether or not Buddhism is pessimistic due to its emphasis on life as suffering and, moreover, the third Truth's teaching of Cessation (*nirodha*), considered as a kind of nihilism. This kind of view can still be found in Christian critiques of Buddhism, although it is no longer witnessed in any serious academic debate. Sometimes in Buddhist teachings, Enlightenment itself is equated with Cessation, and the word *Nirvāṇa* etymologically implies a blowing out or extinction, but understood as an extinction of the fires of the emotional afflic-tions. The use of negatives is explicitly linked to the stark opposition drawn between the suffering of conditioned existence and the total peace of *nirvāṇa*, also called the unconditioned (*asaṃskṛta*).

Whatever conditioned existence is, unconditioned existence is not. How then would it be possible to describe the unconditioned except with the use of negatives? Even if the unconditioned may be replete with amazing features, the language of the conditioned could be considered inappropriate to express this: the only option is to experience it for oneself. Nonetheless, the third Truth's image of Cessation, remaining central as it does in many Buddhist contexts, is also balanced by other presentations which focus on the qualities of wisdom which arise in the wake of the demise of craving and ignorance. For instance, we have noted in Chapter 1 the *Ten Powers of a Tathāgata*, and, later, the development of the vision of the three Buddha bodies, Buddha fields and Buddha nature in Mahāyāna traditions.

A distinction is made between *nirvāṇa* attained during life, when the aggregates of the person are still present, and the nirvāṇa or final nirvāṇa (*parinirvāṇa*) without any remainder, when an enlightened one passes away without being reborn again.

THE TRUTH OF THE WAY TO THE CESSATION OF SUFFERING: THE NOBLE EIGHTFOLD PATH

The fourth Truth spells out how to effect the stopping of craving. This is through the *Middle Way*, which is further broken down into eight aspects: view, resolve, speech, action, livelihood, effort, mindfulness, and meditative absorption. We will look at the individual aspects further below. When these components are perfected, the Path becomes the Noble Path or the Path as practised by the Noble Ones. Each of the eight are described as *samyak*, whole, complete or perfect. The word is the same term which is used in the phrase *samyak-saṃbuddha, completely perfected Buddha*. In the context of the Eightfold Path, it is often translated as 'right', which may not quite give the appropriate nuance if it is thought of as simply implying 'good' or 'correct'. At the risk of overuse, *perfect* might be a better translation.

As mentioned in Chapter 1, the Eightfold Path is symbolised in the Dharma Wheel with eight spokes which connect at the hub and work together. There is also some logic to their ordering, although it is noteworthy that the sequence differs from the most commonly used structuring of the Path in Buddhism into the *Three Trainings* of Moral Discipline, Meditative Absorption, and Wisdom. The standard understandings of the correspondences between the

Eightfold Path and the Three Trainings connects the first two aspects with Wisdom, the next three with Moral Discipline and the final three with Meditative Absorption. The Three Trainings are seen at least to some extent as representing a schema for a gradual development from the beginner stages of ethical training to a culmination with the arising of wisdom. The Eightfold Path, in contrast, starts with the components associated with wisdom, on the grounds that without an appropriate approach and understanding, there is little basis for the following aspects to be perfected. The two formulations are considered entirely consistent since, in both cases, there is also some sense of the various aspects developing simultaneously and interrelating, and, moreover, the Eightfold Path can be thought to revolve, so that the initial wisdom is later deepened. Yet, perhaps, there is a certain slight difference in emphasis. The Three Trainings represent an institutionalised schema considered appropriate for all, whereas perhaps the initial Eightfold Path formulation might have been intended primarily for the committed renouncers, as is the impression given in its presentation within the *Dhammacakkappavattana Sutta*. Be that as it may, generally, in Buddhist teachings, the Eightfold Path and the Three Trainings are integrated entirely comfortably.

The Eightfold Path structure permeates later Buddhism to a greater or lesser extent. It remains central in Southern Buddhism, given the Theravāda tradition's concern of representing the early teachings as faithfully as possible. In Northern and East Asian Buddhism, the eightfold formula as such is rather superseded by later framings of Buddhist practice, such as the six bodhisattva transcendent actions or perfections (*pāramitā*), but the Eightfold Path does not altogether disappear. Its aspects, sometimes re-worked somewhat, can be encountered within the later schemas. For instance, there is a Tibetan tantric system which emphasises a threefold pattern of 'view, meditation and conduct'. Although the term *view* has slightly different connotations in this system, it is, nonetheless, exactly the same term as the first term in the Eightfold Path, and the three aspects can be seen as corresponding to the Three Trainings in reverse order.

THE THREE TRAININGS: I MORAL DISCIPLINE

Moral discipline (*śīla*) is considered to provide a necessary basis for the development of meditation and wisdom. With the avoidance of wrong-doing and especially of the harming of living beings, and with the cultivation of beneficial acts, it is considered that the mind becomes free from remorse and more peaceful, so that meditation can be practised effectively. Moreover, moral discipline is considered to generate much 'merit' or good karma, karmic fruitfulness leading to more positive circumstances, again enabling meditation to bear fruit. But this is not all. There is also an important sense in which moral discipline is considered *in itself* to be an integral part of the spiritual training, not merely a preliminary preparation but an important constituent of the meditative life. The spiritual path is aimed at the reduction and final elimination of craving, and Buddhist morality is directly concerned with this goal through its physical, verbal and mental discipline to curb self-centred desires. Furthermore, mindfulness is necessary in practising moral discipline, in order to recollect the precepts and to identify the desires before they are acted on, and persistent application is needed to maintain the discipline over time. Thus – and we will consider the implications of this in the chapter on the Sangha – maintaining moral discipline is at the heart of the monastics' spiritual practice, as well as that of the laity.

THE THREE TRAININGS AND THE BODHISATTVA PATH

In the Eightfold Path formulation, perfect speech, action and livelihood are classified as the aspects relating to moral discipline. As mentioned above, in Mahāyāna Buddhism, although the early classification was kept intact, rather greater emphasis was put on the six transcendent actions (*pāramitā*) of a bodhisattva. We have seen in Chapter 1 that stories about the heroic deeds of the bodhisattva who aspires for completely perfected buddhahood are common to all Buddhist traditions. The non-Mahāyāna schools, such as the only still extant non-Mahāyāna order, the Theravāda, accept the bodhisattva ideal as the most supreme, but they take the view that it is only appropriate for really exceptional individuals. Just as scientists could not all hope to become Einstein, and they may achieve little if they attempt to do so, so most people are best able to attain Enlightenment by following the path to become enlightened as an *arhat*. The Mahāyāna groups, on the other hand, considered the supreme Enlightenment of a Buddha as a valid ideal for all, and hence they developed the existing traditions on the stages of the bodhisattva path into a systematic list of transcendent actions to be cultivated by all aspiring bodhisattvas. In the most usual list of six, moral discipline (*śīla*) is specifically given as the second, although in the broader sense of the Three Trainings, which are still used in the bodhisattva practice, moral discipline also encompasses the first aspect of generosity (*dāna*) and the third of patience (*kṣānti*). The fourth of diligent application or vigour (*vīrya*) – related to the sixth aspect of the Eightfold Path (perfect effort) – is sometimes also classified under the first Training, although often, as in the Eightfold Path, considered under the heading of Meditative Absorption, or alternatively, even said to be part of all Three Trainings. The final two transcendent actions correspond unproblematically to the second and third Training, that is, deep absorption (*dhyāna*), connected to the broader category of meditative absorption (*samādhi*) and wisdom (*prajñā*), although in Mahāyāna practice their connotations, especially that of wisdom, are rather different.

THE FIVE PRECEPTS

Whether connected with aspects of the Eightfold Path or of the bodhisattva path, moral discipline is linked to the Buddhist precepts to refrain from unwholesome or evil actions, and the most basic list of five applies to lay disciples as well as monastics. In fact, although interpretation differs, the code itself was shared with the Jains, and perhaps with other Renouncer groups. In the Buddhist tradition, the five precepts are usually ceremonially accepted at the time of making the commitment to Buddhism by *Going for Refuge*. They will be ritually chanted after the *Refuge* formula in the presence of a Buddhist teacher or monk, often with the palms folded. They are also recited on other occasions, as a component of regular ritual practice, or on special Dharma practice days, especially in Southern Buddhism, when lay people may visit their local monastery and reaffirm their commitments.

The precepts are broken if the act is performed intentionally and carried through to its conclusion. Here, Buddhism differed from the stricter definitions of other Renouncers such as the Jains, who judged the act in itself to be evil, rather than its deliberate performance. In Buddhism, accidental negative acts are only considered to create bad karma if they are culpably careless. The five precepts are:

(1) Not to take life. This precept is the most fundamental and, in its broadest sense, it implies that one should refrain from in any way harming human, animal or other sentient life. Different forms of killing are related to the different emotional afflictions as classified in Buddhism. Thus, killing enemies or irritating insects, etc. is taking life through hatred or aggression. Killing for food or sport is taking life through desire or greed, and killing in sacrificial rituals, etc. is taking life through delusion. In very early Buddhist texts, there is some indication that the definition of living things could include plant life, as in the Jain tradition, but it was established quite early to draw the line between plants and animals. Thus, lay Buddhists could be farmers. The felling of trees, however, might be avoided where possible on the grounds that spirit beings might be living in and dependent on the trees.

(2) Not to take what is not given. The precept covers stealing, fraud and any form of appropriation without willing agreement of property belonging to others.

(3) Not to speak falsely. Here, the worst breakage is outright lying, but the precept also covers any form of deceptive or misleading speech as well as, more broadly, speaking harshly, divisively, nonsensically or frivolously.   — Homosexuality

(4) Not to indulge in sexual misconduct. This precept implies that sexuality should not involve any exploitation or breaking of trust. Monastics maintain celibacy vows in addition.

(5) Not to indulge in intoxicants which cloud the mind. For monks and nuns, abstention from alcoholic drinks is expected. For lay people, the precept means that one should not indulge in alcoholic drink or other recreational drugs to the extent of becoming intoxicated so that the other precepts might be broken.

Sometimes the first three are considered the root precepts, since the fourth would stem naturally from them, although the fourth is also sometimes given as a root precept. The fifth is rather different, not proscribing action which is inherently evil, but important in helping to maintain the other precepts. In Northern Buddhism, there are options to take less than five precepts: a lay follower should minimally take the first, or could take the first two, three or four. In practice, however, at least the first three are generally given with the Refuge ceremony.

The above order is standard in Northern Buddhism but in the Pāli Canon and Theravāda formulation, the third and fourth precepts are given in reverse order, and the first three (i.e., (1), (2) and (4) of the list above) then correspond to the Eightfold Path's *perfect action*. In all traditions, positive virtues are associated with the opposites of the behaviour to avoid, such as saving life, loving kindness and compassion, generosity and truthfulness.

In practice, situations in life – especially in lay life – may mean that individuals are unable to keep the precepts purely. Strict adherence is an ideal but there is recognition that people may fall short of the ideal. Confession of downfalls and reaffirmation of the precepts is the most usual way of dealing with this. Only in the case of the most severe infractions on the part of monastics is there the greater sanction that the monastic vows are considered broken beyond the possibility of renewal.

THE PRECEPTS AND THE EIGHTFOLD PATH

The Eightfold Path's *perfect speech* corresponds to the precept on refraining from false speech, as well as avoiding other types of wrong speech. *Perfect mindfulness* includes the precept on avoiding alcoholic drinks which lead to heedless behaviour, while *perfect action* relates to the other three precepts. *Perfect livelihood* also follows from the principles of the precepts: one's way of making a living should not harm other beings, nor involve any unfair appropriation, falsehood, etc.

OTHER PRECEPT LISTS

There are longer lists of more specific precepts involving further restraints on self-indulgent activities. These can be taken for specified periods, such as for the course of meditative retreats or religious festivals, or they may be taken on a long-term basis by serious lay followers who are not in a position to take the full monastic vows.

The list of monastic precepts is far longer and much more specific, relating to matters of decorum and socially acceptable behaviour for monks, as well as restraints which relate to actions which would be contrary to the spirit of the basic precepts and thus considered to be of a naturally evil nature. There is much continuity between the precept lists of different monastic ordination lineages although the exact numbers vary. But the main historical disputes over the monastic precepts have not been over their content but their exact interpretation, some schools being more relaxed than others.

There are also lists of precepts associated with the bodhisattva vow to attain the Enlightenment of a buddha for the sake of all living beings. The bodhisattva ethic slightly changes the framing for Buddhist morality, in that it focuses less on self-restraint for the sake of one's own spiritual progress, and more on the benefits for others. Throughout Buddhism, one finds the idea that it is possible to transfer one's own merit to others, or at least share it with them, for example, by performing virtuous actions or religious practice to help relatives or friends. Some Buddhist sources explain the process in terms of encouraging the recipient to rejoice in the virtue, thus benefitting their mental continuum. Alternatively, a ritual dedication of good wishes and offerings may please local gods, who then bestow help, or it may assuage spirit beings, who then desist from harming a sick or deceased person for whom the practice is done. However the effect on the recipient may be explained, a ritualised dedication is considered to have a very real impact, enhancing the positive value of good acts. Tibetan teachings stress that without dedicating virtues, their benefits may be dissipated, or destroyed by subsequent negative impulses. Dedication to others is said to work like adding a drop of water to an ocean, thus preserving it until the ocean runs dry, in contrast to a drop of water evaporating on hot sand.

In bodhisattva practice, all virtue accumulated is systematically dedicated for the Enlightenment of all. The lists of bodhisattva precepts mostly reiterate general Buddhist principles, largely sharing the same definitions of harmful and virtuous acts, although they introduce a trump card of compassion for others. This can have a similar role to Christian teachings on love, which may supersede the earlier Biblical commandments in some cases. The bodhisattva imperative of compassion is found in the pan-Buddhist stories of the Buddha-to-be's previous lives, such as in the popular story of the life when he fed his own body to a hungry tigress thus, in effect, taking his own life. Such extreme heroism is not encouraged by the bodhisattva precepts, but they do include the point that the basic precepts are to be broken in the interests of compassion, such as lying in order to save a life and so forth. Nonetheless, such action tends to be rather hedged in by provisos. Most importantly, a good intention is not generally considered sufficient to justify the breaking of the precepts: compassion needs to be accompanied by wisdom. If the intrinsically negative act turns out to be counterproductive and in fact causes harm, such as the assassination of a tyrant, which leads to a backlash of further killing and repression, this would not be considered to be good bodhisattva activity. So, one needs the wisdom of discernment to distinguish between genuinely compassionate and helpful acts and those which merely appear to be so, or reflect a misplaced emotional desire to be of service.

Tantric Buddhism adds a further list of precepts called *samaya* vows. These focus on maintaining the tantric vision and the coherence of the community of tantric practitioners. Again, much of the code of conduct is in line with other Buddhist practice, especially Mahāyāna approaches, but some versions of these vows contain apparent inversions of the basic precepts. Generally, however, such inversions act as powerful psychological mechanisms for using the impulses of the emotional afflictions to uproot those afflictions, such as a precept to 'kill' ignorant thoughts with the knife of pure awareness, etc. In Northern Buddhism, there are debates about how the different sets of precepts should be integrated, and varied ideas about which is to be prioritised in the case of a conflict.

PRACTISING VIRTUE: GENEROSITY

The first of the bodhisattva transcendent actions, giving or generosity (*dāna*), is also an important practice in non-Mahāyāna Buddhism, considered to create much virtue and long-term merit which can be taken from one life to the next. Giving is often said to be of three kinds: the giving of material things, of protection, and of teaching. In the case of the giving of material things, it is considered meritorious to give to those in most need. At the same time, the merit generated is considered to be greatest if the recipient is a monastic so that the gift supports religious practice. Perhaps the single most fundamental feature of lay Buddhist practice in much of Asia is the laity's expression of the Buddhist virtue of generosity through showing respect and through giving food and other support to the monastic Sangha. In accepting the offerings, the monastics provide an opportunity for lay people to generate merit. They may also reciprocate through the giving of teaching, considered the highest kind of giving. The funding of buddha images, of the copying of textual manuscripts or their printing, of the building of Buddhist shrines and temples, and the sponsorship of public religious rituals are all considered worthy gifts, which may bring some recognition in the community as well as longer-term merit. A serious obstacle for the development of Buddhism in Western countries is that large-scale funding necessary for the support of monasteries and full-time religious practitioners has been less readily available, partly because, as a tiny minority religion, the social support is absent, and partly because Western followers may take a more individualistic approach to their religion rather than fund public religious projects.

In the bodhisattva practice, transcendent giving implies entirely unselfish giving with no thought of return, even of merit for oneself, and with a view that makes no distinction between the giver and the recipient seeing them both, along with the act of giving, as empty in their nature. Yet, such truly selfless giving is considered to generate the greatest merit!

THE APPLICATION OF BUDDHIST ETHICAL PRINCIPLES IN SOCIAL LIFE

As discussed at the beginning of the chapter, even in principle, there is the recognition that rather different approaches may all have some value, perhaps at different stages of the spiritual path. Yet, at the same time, there is a clear and universally applicable ethical code in Buddhism, especially regarding not killing or harming sentient beings. In many respects, then, we can expect to find fairly clear-cut ethical positions, for example, on matters concerning the treatment of animals, or threats to human life including abortion, warfare, and so on. However, clear-cut ethical positions do not always translate into hard-line value judgements – let alone legislative interference, etc. – for a very important reason.

In mainstream Buddhist doctrine, we find a clear dichotomy between the 'worldly' and the spiritual life, and the metaphor for entry into the religious vocation is that of 'going forth' from the householder life embroiled in worldly concerns to the 'homeless' status of the monastic. The contrast between the two modes of life is brought out in the doctrinal opposition between the endless miserable cycle of *saṃsāra* and the peace and bliss of its cessation in *nirvāṇa*. Symbolically, the *saṃsāra/nirvāṇa* and the worldly house-holder/monk divides are connected. Monks are meant to represent the values of the 'homeless life', including its universalistic ethical code, but the affairs of householders are not the monk's concern. This means that some areas of social life which elsewhere would come under the domain of religion are considered 'worldly' or, in today's parlance, secular matters in Buddhist contexts.

In this respect, Buddhism can be seen as contrasting with other religions and perhaps especially with Islam. Muslim doctrine assumes that the religion has the duty to engage itself closely with many aspects of secular life, both public affairs and community, kinship and family matters. Religious injunctions relating to such areas as economic life, social justice, feuding, criminal law, marriage, inheritance, and correct behaviour for men and for women are specified at length in scripture itself and elaborated upon further by the major traditions of religious law. In contrast, in principle and to a considerable extent in practice, Buddhist monastics and other specialists should refrain from interference in large areas of secular life. This is not to say that the Buddhist Dharma is divorced from everyday life or community concerns. On the contrary, upright ethical action in keeping with Buddhist values is enjoined for all, and is especially emphasised for those in positions of authority in society. But in Buddhism, monks and nuns (as perhaps, in some orders of Christian monks) are forbidden by monastic discipline from many kinds of involvements in 'worldly' affairs.

Traditionally, Buddhist monks may play little role in social rites-de-passage, with the exception of funerals, which are their specialism. Recitations and rituals may be performed for the benefit of the departed, and funerals also provide ample opportunity for reflection on the Buddhist understanding of impermanence. But other rites-de-passage may have very little Buddhist context at all. There are no Buddhist rules or specifications about appropriate or allowable marriage systems, no pronouncements on divorce, and so on. Asian Buddhist societies had a range of different marriage arrangements without the religion having a problem. Within Tibetan contexts, several types of marriage were possible until modern times, including cohabitation and non-resident partnerships, and this was not a topic on which the religious specialists would be expected to comment. Even in the case of abortion, where the Buddhist moral position is clear, considering human life to begin at conception, it is not always considered appropriate for monks to interfere or lobby for secular mechanisms to limit or prohibit terminations. Religious figures such as the Dalai Lama may be more likely to lament the sad circumstances of life which might seem to make abortion a lesser of two evils, than to be judgemental or to promote strict laws. In Thailand, the Buddhist order's opposition to abortion has been a significant factor in its legal restriction. But in other cases, the absence of any strong lobby from the Buddhist establishment is striking, considering its clear ethical objection to abortion. Instead, there may be concern to develop awareness of the issue from a Buddhist perspective, as well as spiritual support for those who have been personally involved, including the provision of rites for aborted foetuses.

In the past century, there have been some modifications of the traditional attitude that monastics should be aloof from social concerns. For instance, 'Buddhist' weddings have been developed and, more significantly, monk involvement in social work and community activism. This is especially notable in Southern Buddhism. In Sri Lanka, it is related to the kinds of developments which have been referred to as 'Buddhist Modernism' or 'Protestant Buddhism', in part stimulated by Christian missionary criticism of Buddhist uninvolvement in the social world. It is also linked to the need for new monastic roles in a modern context where the traditional support systems have been undermined. But although such developments are playing a part in creative adaptations to contemporary life, ironically, in general, Buddhism's long-term survival might be more secure if the more traditional approach of avoiding lay concerns were upheld. Given the pace and extent of social and technological change, a religious tradition may find it has problems if it is too precise about expected behaviour norms, and Buddhism's clear position that the religion should not interfere with secular matters fits well with a modern value system.

BUDDHIST APPROACHES TO MORAL DILEMMAS: A CASE STUDY OF MEAT EATING

The five precepts provide a set of general principles to act as guidelines in moral decision-making, but it may not be so easy to interpret them for specific situations. This is especially so where a strict interpretation may be impractical for most people and also where there might seem to be some conflict between the precepts and other Buddhist virtues such as loving kindness and compassion as, for instance, when a sentient being is in severe terminal pain so that it might seem kinder to take its life.

The far more specific monastic rules may give rather more clear guidance, but it is not straightforward to translate monastic rules into guidelines for lay practice. To take the example of the monastic rules regarding the consumption of meat, a monk should not accept meat which he knows or suspects to have been killed especially for him, and he should also check that any meat given to him is not of one of the prohibited meats such as human flesh and wild animal flesh, meats considered inappropriate by the wider society. This rule seems to have been related to the Middle Way approach: strict vegetarianism for all monks might put too much pressure on the lay community to cook specially for monks, but monastics are not to be responsible for any life being taken, nor for encouraging meat eating. Although vegetarianism was not insisted on for monks, it remained an option for monastics wishing to practise more strictly.

Monks' rules are generally stricter than what would be expected for lay people. Historically, many Buddhists have considered that if vegetarianism was not even necessary for monks, lay people could hardly be expected to adopt it. So long as they are not personally responsible for the animal's death, they need not see themselves as guilty of taking life. However, one difficulty in extending the monastic rule to any general principle applicable to the lay community is that it rests on the assumption that the monk is not generally making choices about his food since he is dependent on lay provision, an assumption not applicable to lay people. The rule implies that vegetarian food is less harmful, and the only allowable reason for a monk to accept meat is when it is merely left-over food which would anyway have been prepared. Thus, an alternative view is that a lay person who exercises choice would seem to entail some responsibility for the animal's death by deliberately choosing meat. A number of important Mahāyāna texts took the view that, even for monks, it is never possible for meat to satisfy the condition that one has no responsibility for taking the life. After all, even if lay people may appear to be giving a monk left-overs, they may in fact have prepared the food in the knowledge that they would be offering part of the meal to the monk and made their choices accordingly.

As mentioned above, in Mahāyāna doctrine the principle of compassion can override the basic rules. Thus, in the case of meat eating, another argument found in Mahāyāna sources is that the early monks' rule should in any case be overridden by compassion for the animal. Even if a monk is not personally responsible for the death, a bodhisattva's compassion for sentient beings should be like that of a mother who could not bear to consume the flesh of her own children. Although the doctrine of compassion is developed explicitly in Mahāyāna scriptures, it would, however, be a mistake to assume that it is only in Mahāyāna contexts where such arguments would have validity. In fact, teachings on loving kindness, generally defined as wishing sentient beings to be happy, and compassion, defined as wishing for sentient beings to be free from suffering, are pan-Buddhist virtues and may also be emphasised by some non-Mahāyāna teachers.

Similar considerations and a range of views apply to other cases of moral dilemmas. The limitations of practicality are also significant in identifying the Middle Way in specific situations, which may vary in time and place. Thus, in our above example, in practice, even though Mahāyāna traditions would seem to favour a stricter interpretation of the precept of not taking life in relation to food, in most Asian Buddhist countries, vegetarianism was a practical option only for the most ascetic. While in East Asian Buddhism, monks and nuns are generally vegetarian and religious festivals usually entail vegetarian foods, in Tibet, where there are limited protein-rich non-meat sources and fruits and vegetables are difficult to grow, vegetarianism was generally limited to the more ascetic hermits.

In contemporary contexts, greater communication between different Buddhist traditions, and between Buddhist and non-Buddhist communities, has increased reflexivity about Asian practices. One effect of this is that there has been more debate over appropriate Buddhist responses to ethical issues, especially those which are topical in today's world, such as environmental concerns and animal rights. In relation to our case study of the ethics of food, there are now Buddhist movements promoting vegetarianism, such as one amongst Tibetan exiles in India, living in a country where religious vegetarianism in Hinduism and Jainism has long been established and food choices broader than in pre-modern Tibet. But a good deal of the impetus in such developments owes at least as much to 'traditional' thinking as to modern adaptations. For instance, one influential lama who has adopted and promoted vegetarianism has stated that he was initially prompted by concerns over 'obstacles' to his life. In traditional Buddhist teaching, longevity is linked with the saving of life so students can help prolong the master's life by vegetarianism. Most lamas who have become involved in vegetarianism may mention, say, the Indian context where Tibetans may be put to shame by Indian vegetarians, but the primary justifications they have drawn on include the textual heritage of famous hermit lamas who encouraged vegetarianism, as well as Mahāyāna scriptural sources.

THE THREE TRAININGS: II MEDITATIVE ABSORPTION

The second training of meditative absorption (*samādhi*) is central throughout mainstream Buddhist traditions and is not confined to a few virtuoso practitioners living in retreat, although specialist meditators do play an important part in preserving the heritage of meditative practices associated with advanced spiritual accomplishment. But 'meditative absorption' is a broader category than the idea some English language readers may have of hours of still and silent meditation. In fact it can include a wide range of practices, such as the meditative recitation of liturgies perhaps to musical accompaniment, or practices combining inner contemplation with outer activities such as 'walking meditation', in which the meditator becomes absorbed in awareness of all the bodily movements and interaction with the environment. At its broadest, it can also include popular practices such as circumambulation of sacred sites or monuments, or the Northern Buddhist practice of reciting *mantra*s or sacred strings of tantric syllables accompanied by repetitive turning of '*mantra* wheels', cylindrical constructions revolving around a central spindle and containing written *mantra*s.

There are so many types of meditation in the different traditions of Buddhism that we can do little more here than to review a few of them and look at some of the general principles. Meditative training can involve virtually any practice which focuses the mind and deepens awareness, ideally so that the power of the emotional afflictions to overwhelm the mind is reduced, and an inner experience of tranquillity, happiness and clarity is engendered. It would be incorrect to think that Buddhism lacks clearly articulated beliefs or practices based on faith or devotional worship. Yet it is true that in theory, and often in practice too, there is less interest in insistence on correct beliefs or acceptance of religious authorities than in encouragement to practise meditation and mind training, and to gain understanding for oneself. There are quite clear notions about what will be discovered and what the various stages of discovery imply, so it is not that the follower is urged to find their own truth but, rather, to make the truth their own.

While it is clear that meditative practices pervade much everyday Buddhist ritual, it is also the case that to practise meditative absorption in a manner which is considered necessary to produce significant spiritual attainment generally demands an intensive full-time commitment, perhaps in a retreat or monastic environment with few distractions over a period of years. This kind of intensive long-term mind training may also bring the practitioner face-to-face with previously subliminal psychological fixations, sadness, inadequacies, and so forth, or may give rise to apparently spiritual or paranormal experiences which may not be straightforward to interpret. Furthermore, there may be times when the apprentice meditator may lack the discernment to carry out the meditation instructions properly. For instance, there are times when the mind may be over-excited and techniques for relaxing it may be necessary, and other times when the mind is sluggish and needs to be roused using opposite tactics. For these reasons, it is usually considered vital for meditation training to be carried out under the guidance of an experienced teacher, with the student regularly consulting the teacher, who checks the student's practice and suggests modifications.

THE BRAHMĀ ABODES (BRAHMA-VIHĀRAS)

One important and popular meditation practice is known as the *Brahmā Abodes* or the four *Immeasurables*. The name is related to early texts about the set (such as the *Subha Sutta* found in the *Majjhima Nikāya* (MN 99) or the *Digha Nikāya*'s *Tevijjā Sutta* DN 13) in which the Buddha is questioned about how to ensure finding the divine abode of Brahmā. The Buddha explains that the way to ensure such a divine birth is to practise loving kindness, compassion, sympathetic joy, and equanimity. The technique, explained in many sources, is to meditate on each in turn, pervading the world in all directions with thoughts of loving kindness, free from anger and ill will, and then to repeat the process with the other three.

The mainstream Buddhist tradition, witnessed both in Theravāda and Mahāyāna sources, has interpreted the Brahmā abodes as indicating one of the highest heavenly realms, where the brahmā deities reside. Thus, this meditation practice is not usually thought to lead directly to Enlightenment, although one modern scholar has suggested that the term may rather have been intended as a synonym for Enlightenment. Even from the viewpoint of the standard interpretation, it is clear that the practice is believed to bring both short-term benefits in terms of greater peace and empathy with others as well as significant spiritual progress.

TRANQUILLITY AND INSIGHT MEDITATION

One important classification of meditation systems in Buddhism is the distinction between tranquillity (*śamatha*) and insight (*vipaśyanā*) meditation. Some meditative techniques are classified as wholly one or the other, while others integrate the two, or use tranquillity meditation to establish a calm single-pointed mind and then insight meditation to develop penetrating awareness. Both feature in the early stories of the Buddha's journey to Enlightenment. The attainments of tranquillity meditation correspond to the system of the four progressively-staged deep absorptions described as the basis for the Buddha's final meditations on the night of his Enlightenment (see Chapter 1), while the three knowledges which were said to arise following this would correspond to the fruition of insight meditation. In the Eightfold Path's list of aspects, *perfect meditative absorption* is more closely associated with tranquillity meditation. *Mindfulness* is also needed for tranquillity meditation but more associated with developing insight, which becomes *perfect view*. In relation to the Buddhist objective of undermining the fundamental causal process engendering continued suffering, tranquillity meditation is more concerned with pacifying craving, while insight leads to wisdom which cuts off ignorance.

Varying approaches to the two types of meditation are witnessed from the early texts. On the one hand, presentations emphasising the development of the deep absorptions, which are associated with tranquillity, may give the impression that wisdom arises rather naturally out of the calm and clear single-pointed mind after one has mastered the absorptions. On the other hand, some presentations emphasising the development of mindfulness say little or nothing about the deep absorptions, implying that so long as one's mind is focused enough to maintain mindful awareness of physical and mental processes, and the factors associated with spiritual progress, this is sufficient to develop the insight necessary to become enlightened. However, it is perhaps more typical for Buddhist traditions to combine or at least to offer training in both methods, and both are represented in the Eightfold Path and in the bodhisattva six transcendent acts, where the fifth act develops deep absorption while the sixth, transcendent wisdom, encompasses the perfection of insight.

Both tranquillity and insight meditation can have 'supports' or be 'without supports'. Meditations without supports are those which do not require any focus other than, for example, the breathing, while meditations with supports include contemplations on Buddha images or meditations using set recitations, and so forth. In either case, tranquillity practices will tend to focus the attention on one point, to calm down discursive thoughts, desires and emotional turmoil, and to lead to states of concentrated absorptions, peace and contentment. Insight meditations, in contrast, may do little to stem the flow of thoughts or to limit awareness on a single point. Rather, they develop mindful penetrating clarity through observing the movements of the mind and looking directly into the nature of the processes of phenomena arising and passing away. However, it is generally considered to be necessary to have reached a certain degree of meditative stability through developing tranquillity to some extent as a basis for insight.

SELF-POWER/OTHER-POWER CONTRASTS

A rather different kind of contrast between different types of meditation in Buddhism can be brought out by a classification sometimes used in East Asian Buddhist traditions but which can be seen as more widely applicable, between approaches which emphasise 'self-power' and those which emphasise 'other-power'. 'Self-power' indicates meditative practice entailing a good deal of self-discipline and application. Japanese Zen Buddhist practice is often seen as typical of 'self-power', involving long hours of sitting meditation and other disciplines. On the other hand, 'other-power' is associated with traditions such as the Pure Land schools, focusing on the worship of the Buddha Amitābha (= Amida, see Chapter 1). In this case, it is faith which is engendered, and the repetitive chanting of Amida's name simply calls upon Amida's saving grace.

Mostly in Buddhist meditation systems, there is some balance between *self-power* and *other-power*. Even practices which most stress individual striving to develop insight may have some element of *other-power*, even if it may simply consist of preliminary making of obeisance, and recitations of praises to the Three Jewels and of *Going for Refuge*. The approaches and practices which seem typical for the mainstream Buddhist traditions drawing inspiration from the formulations of the Eightfold Path or the bodhisattva transcendent activities tend to lean more towards the pole of *self-power* in their emphasis on the need for persistent application on the spiritual path. In the classic imagery of the physician's prescription, the diagnosis of the first Truth and its cause is outlined by the Buddha who is the doctor, supplying also the prescription of the third and fourth Truths, but the student must accept and take the medicine, following through the course of the treatment.

However, *self-power* alone may be considered to risk egocentric distortions of the spiritual path. It is considered necessary to put trust in the Three Jewels, and to have faith and confidence in the Buddhist teachings, especially in the initial stages of the path. Practices such as regular ritual bowing and prostrations before buddha images or senior Buddhist teachers are found in most Buddhist traditions. Such practices often go beyond formalities, becoming integrated into meditative training, such as in the 'extraordinary foundation practices' of Northern Buddhism, which include one hundred thousand full-length prostrations before a visualised buddha figure surrounded by further representations of the Three Jewels. There are also contemplations on the inspiring qualities of the Buddha or, in Mahāyāna practice, of buddhas of other world systems. All such practices could be seen as relying on *other-power* to some extent, even though they still generally entail an element of individual application. Reliance solely on *other-power* is mostly considered inadequate for final Enlightenment, even in Pure Land Buddhism. In Pure Land practice, reliance on *other-power* achieves rebirth in Amida's Pure Land. Once there, circumstances will be conducive for developing the meditation and wisdom needed to attain full Enlightenment.

MONASTIC CHANTING AND RITUAL PRACTICES

Solitary meditation has an important place in Buddhism, but a large majority of monks and nuns live in monastic communities and may spend much of their time performing communal monastic religious rites and ritual recitations for lay people. As noted above, these rituals may be considered an important part of meditative training. The efficacy of such rituals, however, may be considered to be related to the meditative skills of the practitioners. Thus, lay people with a choice will generally prefer to sponsor monks known to be experienced or accomplished meditators to perform rites for them rather than, say, a group of novices who may merely have learnt the outer recitations. The irony for monastic communities specialising in advanced meditation training is that they may be more in demand for the performance of regular rituals than monasteries more explicitly providing a basic monastic training and catering for the lay community. This may even become a problem threatening to interrupt the primary focus of the meditative community. Specialist meditators may therefore retreat to reclusive locations, such as forest hermitages in Southern Buddhism or mountain retreats in Northern Buddhism. For the most part, however, monastic communities will be closely connected with lay settlements in the area, from which they may recruit monks and receive support.

Some communal rituals relate to the monastic code, such as the ordination ceremony and the regular communal recitation of the monastic precepts. There may be a great many other regular rituals depending on the tradition. A common practice throughout the Buddhist world is the chanting of texts, including Buddhist scriptures or other holy liturgies, either in an Indian Buddhist language such as Pāli or Sanskrit, or in vernacular languages. In either case, the recitations will frequently be in verse form, and often chanted in melodic tones, sometimes with musical accompaniment or time keeping. Such recitations may involve similar kinds of meditative techniques to those of the more formal meditation methods, including focused awareness on the meaning and calming the mind or becoming absorbed through the repetitive chanting method.

The chanting of texts and other Buddhist rituals may be sponsored by lay people, as a way of generating merit which can be directed towards or shared with the lay sponsor or their family, perhaps due to ill health or other troubles. There may also be rituals for specific purposes which lay people may request monks to perform, either increasing auspiciousness and success or creating protection. It is a mistake to assume that such practices are inevitably at odds with the early Buddhist favouring of reasoned argument and rejection of meaningless ritual. Early Buddhism had various strands, which included the incorporation of ritual symbolism in keeping with Buddhist ethics and doctrinal approaches. Early Buddhist rituals expressed a range of attitudes towards animals and spirit beings within nature, drawing to a greater or lesser extent on ancient Vedic ritual manipulation. One theme is the application of meditative contemplation of friendliness and loving kindness, but, even in very early sources, this may be backed up by truth magic in which the fulfilment of the desired outcome depends on a ritual assertion of the truth, in Buddhist contexts, of the supreme qualities of the Buddha and his teaching. Another approach is the use of magical formulae to invoke protection, a technique which persists in many Buddhist countries and which was later taken up by the tantras, and is especially witnessed in Northern Buddhist contexts.

THE THREE TRAININGS: III WISDOM

The third training of wisdom (*prajñā*) is the spiritual path's culmination leading to Enlightenment. Its development is considered to depend on conceptual or intellectual understanding, including an appreciation of the four Truths, the processes of karma, and so forth. This level of understanding needs to be deepened through the development of insight in meditative training, while the final realisation implies direct perception of the nature of reality. Thus, both conceptual understanding and meditative insight are necessary in the Buddhist Wisdom training, although there may be significant differences in the weighting given to meditative insight or intellectual training amongst different groups, even within a single Buddhist tradition.

In the Eightfold Path formulation, the first two aspects, *perfect view* and *perfect resolve*, relate to Wisdom. In the early stages of the spiritual path, *perfect view* is to approach life in terms of karma and rebirth and then the four Truths, seeing conditioned existence in terms of suffering, impermanence and not-self, and recognising the path to liberation. *Perfect resolve* is then the persistent determination to act in accordance with this view. It includes renunciation of worldly goals and a motivation to bring benefit rather than harm to oneself and others. The Noble transcendent versions of the two aspects imply direct understanding and application of that understanding, leading to the three knowledges which marked the Buddha's Enlightenment or, at least, the third knowledge which all Arhats are said to attain.

THE PROCESS OF KARMA: THE DEPENDENTLY ARISING LINKS

FORMULA OF DEPENDENT ARISING

From ignorance comes volitional activities. From volitional activities comes consciousness. From consciousness comes mind and body. From mind and body come the six sense faculties. From the six sense faculties comes contact. From contact comes feeling. From feeling comes craving. From craving comes grasping. From grasping comes becoming. From becoming comes birth. From birth, comes aging and death ... Such is the origination of this whole mass of suffering.

By the destruction of ignorance, volitional activities are destroyed. By the destruction of volitional activities, consciousness is destroyed. By the destruction of consciousness, mind and body are destroyed. By the destruction of mind and body, the six sense faculties are destroyed. By the destruction of the six sense faculties, contact is destroyed. By the destruction of contact, feeling is destroyed. By the destruction of feeling, craving is destroyed. By the destruction of craving, grasping is destroyed. By the destruction of grasping, becoming is destroyed. By the destruction of becoming, birth is destroyed. By the destruction of birth, ageing and death are destroyed. Such is the cessation of this whole mass of suffering.

(Repeated with variations throughout Buddhist scriptural sources.)

IGNORANCE

The discussion of the four Truths above has introduced the Buddhist perspective on causation. It is noteworthy that the first link *ignorance* (*avidyā*) is the opposite of the direct knowledges (*vidyā*) of a buddha, and is the primal evil in Buddhism. Although they may occasionally be equated, there is generally a distinction between this basic ignorance and delusion (*moha*), which is one of the three central emotional afflictions (together with hatred and desire or greed) springing from ignorance. Delusion implies a state of dullness, confusion or stupidity, but ignorance may rather be seen as almost clever or tricky, a wilful failure to see or a deliberate misconstruing of the evidence. A good example of the kind of process which Buddhist thinking on ignorance seems to suggest might be an occasion when I received the sad news of a friend's death some years ago. As I looked at the envelope, and even as I began to open and look at the card notifying me of the funeral (admittedly in a foreign language), for at least a minute or two any thought that the card might concern my friend, who I knew to be ill, was banished as my mind actively raced through and grasped at other possibilities, some extremely unlikely, of who the message related to and what it meant. In Buddhist thinking, this kind of active mental blocking out of the unsavoury truth is seen as being at the root of our experience of life, fundamentally conditioning mental fabrications and related *volitional activities* which create habit patterns, and the resultant *consciousness*, which are the following links.

THE AGGREGATES OF PERSONALITY AND THE NOT-SELF DOCTRINE

The teachings on Dependent Arising are considered to elaborate on the second and third Truth in a manner which demonstrates the processes of life – and liberation from them – without any need to introduce any creator or created being with a fixed identity or 'self'. In fact, falsely clinging to a self is part of the problem of *grasping* or attachment, which arises from *Craving*. This does not mean that individuals do not exist, simply that their personalities are not fixed selves but ever-changing *aggregates* (*skandha*s) of forms, feelings, perceptions, volitions and consciousness. In treating such components as though they represent an unchanging 'self', suffering is exacerbated, since a self-cherishing approach may give rise to non-virtuous acts which harm others and may harm oneself in the longer term, while the person's present combination of features and processes is in any case impermanent, so the cherishing of a self will be ultimately futile. Buddhist sources speak of the personality as a *continuum* or a *stream of consciousness*. Habit patterns may be set up which can persist even from life to life, and the seeds of karma created now may bring good or bad fruit in the future, so that there is causal continuity, but none of this indicates any kind of unchanging personal identity or 'self'.

It should also be appreciated that the Buddhist idea of a false imputation of a 'self' need not indicate a purely conceptual mis-interpretation. Many animals could not create any theory of a 'self', yet, from a Buddhist perspective, they share the *ignorance* of an emotional or psychological approach which takes what is imper-manent, unsatisfactory and not-self as though it were permanent, satisfactory and having self-nature. An important feature of many meditation practices focusing on undercutting ignorance is an extended examination of the body and the mind, discovering that all the components are not-self. Further intellectual analysis of the changing components of animate and inanimate existence also became a preoccupation of Buddhist philosophy, and different sys-tems of classification of these components or *dharma*s can be found in the collections of *Abhidharma* (Higher Teachings) scriptures preserved by the different early Buddhist schools.

TRANSCENDENT WISDOM IN MAHĀYĀNA BUDDHISM

Mahāyāna Buddhism did not jettison early Buddhist understandings of wisdom but, rather, integrated them into a broader under-standing which introduced the idea of a *transcendent wisdom*. This transcendent wisdom of a bodhisattva develops an early Buddhist idea of the emptiness of *dharma*s or the components which combine to form people and things. The main thrust of mainstream Buddhist doctrine, as we have seen, is that such combinations of *dharma*s are empty of any fixed self. The Mahāyāna tradition took up a rather more radical understanding of this emptiness doctrine, one which may already have been present within an important branch of the early Buddhist tradition known as the Mahāsaṃghika. This understanding is that not only are the combinations of *dharma*s which we recognise as persons and things marked by emptiness, but that those individual *dharma*s themselves are empty of any real identity. The Mahāyāna texts seem in particular to challenge the version of Buddhist philosophy associated with the *Sarvāstivāda* school, which was an important tradition in Northern India when the Mahāyāna took shape. Specifically, the Sarvāstivāda school – whose name means, 'the position that everything exists' – held that the different *dharma*s are marked by distinguishing features which have real underlying identities.

Mahāyāna thinking continues: all the components of conditioned existence are empty of any intrinsic nature, but unconditioned existence or *nirvāṇa* similarly lacks any intrinsic nature. Hence, if both are empty, then there is no real difference between them in their ultimate nature. This creates the paradox of the visionary early Mahāyāna *Prajñāpāramitā* (*Transcendent Wisdom*) *sūtra* literature: ultimately, the Buddhist opposition between *saṃsāra* and *nirvāṇa* collapses but, relatively, dependent arising, the four Truths and progress within the bodhisattva path continue to have validity.

The Mahāyāna approach to wisdom is related to its approach to the nature of the Buddha, which we have looked at in Chapter 1. Here we have the denial of any real contrast between the Buddha appearing in the world and a Buddha's disappearance in the final nirvāṇa. This is the basis for the idea that the Buddha may manifest throughout the universe and that our world is actually a buddha field, if only we could clear our defilements and see it.

CHAPTER SUMMARY

- The *Buddha-Dharma* is the Buddha's teachings and the truth expressed by them.
- As a spiritual path, Buddhism is universalistic but still encompasses much variation.
- New teachings may be classified as Dharma if they meet certain criteria.
- The influential four *Truths of the Noble Ones* identify suffering, its cause as craving, its cessation in liberation, and the Noble Eightfold Path.
- Throughout mainstream Buddhism, the spiritual path is divided into the Three Trainings of Moral Discipline, Meditative Absorption, and Wisdom.

- The five precepts and other lists of precepts are important in teachings on moral discipline, which act as a basis for spiritual development but may also constitute that development by reducing craving and non-virtuous acts, and increasing beneficial acts.
- Buddhism's ethical universalism is tempered by the principle that monastics should provide spiritual guidance but not interfere with many areas of secular life, and detailed monastic rules are not always easy to translate into moral principles for lay affairs.
- Meditative absorption is a broad category, not only concerning silent meditation but many everyday practices although intensive meditation is an ideal.
- The distinction between *tranquillity* and *insight meditation* is one important classification of meditation; communal monastic rituals of many types may contribute to meditative training.
- Wisdom is connected to understanding the processes of cause and effect as described in the teachings on dependent arising; in Mahāyāna Buddhism, *transcendent wisdom* adds a rather different perspective.

FURTHER READING

Gethin, Rupert 1998 *The Foundations of Buddhism*. Introduces the fundamentals of Buddhist thinking and practice underlying all the mainstream Buddhist schools, with most focus on Theravāda and Southern Buddhism.

Harvey, Peter 1990 *An Introduction to Buddhism: Teachings, History and Practices*. A wide-ranging survey of Buddhist history, doctrines and practices.

Lopez, Donald (ed.) 1995 *Buddhism in Practice*. An anthology of short textual extracts from a range of traditions.

Williams, Paul 2008 *Mahāyāna Buddhism. The Doctrinal Foundations*. An introduction to Mahāyana approaches.

Williams, Paul and Anthony Tribe 2000 *Buddhist Thought: A Complete Introduction to the Indian Tradition*. As the title suggests, a comprehensive book on Indian Buddhist philosophy.

THE THREE TRAININGS

Harvey, Peter 2000 *An Introduction to Buddhist Ethics: Foundations, Values and Issues*. A detailed exploration of Buddhist ethics, its doctrinal bases and a number of case studies, including consideration of contrasting perspectives in different schools.

Khyentse Rinpoche, Dilgo 2006 *Zurchungpa's Testament*. A traditional treatment of the three trainings from a Tibetan source.

SCRIPTURAL SOURCES

Bullitt, John 2009 *Access to Insight: Readings in Theravada Buddhism* www. accesstoinsight.org/. Try searching the subject index for Pāli scriptural extracts.

Conze, Edward 1973 *The Perfection of Wisdom in Eight Thousand Lines and its Verse Summary*. Translation of key Mahāyāna sūtras on transcendent wisdom.

3

THE TEXTUAL HERITAGE AND ORAL TRANSMISSION

THE IMPORTANCE OF THE CORPUS OF *BUDDHA WORD*

In one Buddhist tradition, notably preserved in the later East Asian Chan (= Japanese Zen) schools, the Buddha named one of his principal students, Mahākāśyapa, as his successor. However, a rather different and influential tradition has it that the Buddha did not appoint a human successor and instead advised his students to rely on the teachings after he passed away: 'It may be, Ananda, that to some among you the thought will come: "Ended is the word of the Master; we have a Master no longer." But it should not, Ananda, be so considered. For that which I have proclaimed and made known as the Dhamma and the Discipline, that shall be your Master when I am gone' (the Theravāda *Mahāparinibbāna Sutta* DN 16). Whatever the truth of the account, from the viewpoint of the Buddhist tradition from the earliest times, the Buddha's teachings were considered the representative or even the embodiment of the Buddha. As we have seen in Chapter 1, Vakkali is reassured that personal meetings are not necessary because the Buddha and his teaching could be equated: 'He who sees the Dhamma, sees me; he who sees me, sees the Dhamma' (*Vakkali Sutta* SN 22.87). The preservation and continuity of what became known as *Buddha*

Word, or scripture, has always therefore been a vital task for the Buddhist community.

In some ways, this was a similar legacy to that of the tenth Sikh Guru, Guru Gobind Singh, in the early eighteenth century. In a context in which his own young sons had been killed and it was clear that any individual human guru was liable to be targeted, Guru Gobind Singh recognised the Sikh holy scriptures, along with the community, as his successor. The sacred status of the holy book was thus elevated to a new height, and worshipping and caring for the *Guru Granth Sahib* became a preoccupation of the Sikh community.

One obvious difference between the two cases is that the eighteenth-century Sikhs had a definite object to treat as their holy scriptures; Guru Gobind Singh had himself prepared an edition which became the basis for the later authorised version. In the early period of Buddhism after the Buddha's passing, in contrast, a priority was to agree exactly what constituted the Dharma. In any case, it implied more than the scriptures alone, in the sense of the *meaning* of the teaching, the truth which is to be realised through the practice of the Path. The meditative traditions, and those of reclusive hermits, have tended to put their main efforts on realisation of the *spirit* rather than the *letter* of the teaching, and there is the idea, for instance in the Chan tradition (at least from the twelfth century CE), of representing a transmission outside the texts. But even in such cases, matters were rarely straightforward. The meditative currents often made use of texts, especially as part of meditative recitation practice, and also in the form of meditation handbooks and guidance notes.

ORAL TRANSMISSION OF THE TEACHINGS

For mainstream Buddhism, clarifications personally given by teacher to students were also important and supplemented the content of the scriptures, but establishing and transmitting the Buddha Word was a central task for the community as a whole. Indeed, the first and subsequent gatherings of the Buddhist community after the Buddha's passing away were convened precisely for 'communal recitations' of the holy texts so that agreement could be reached on this vital matter. In the early period, the scriptures were themselves preserved orally, so the word *scriptures*, used here for *Buddha Word*, is broader than the narrow use of the term to imply written documents alone. The Vedic tradition had techniques for such oral preservation of sacred texts, and the Buddhists developed their own schools of reciters on the basis of similar methods. This had important implications for the style of the early scriptures.

The teachings were codified in ways which are easier to memorise. Although the Pāli *sutta* (discourses) and *vinaya* texts on monastic discipline are by no means insignificant in length, they tend to be rather more succinct in comparison with later written sources. One finds a frequent use of numbered lists, of repetition, and of metrical verse structures which can be recited or chanted.

The readiness with which the scriptures could be recited is not only useful from the point of view of text preservation. Recitation of scriptures and other texts also became a significant aspect of everyday religious instruction and regular practice, and has remained so in Buddhist monasteries across Asia, despite the prevalence of writing for many centuries. Most trainee monks will still be expected to memorise large sections of texts and to recite them communally on a regular basis. Such intimate familiarisation with the texts is expected to establish the teachings more firmly in the mind than is possible by mere occasional reading. As we have seen in the chapter above, ritual chanting of familiar texts in the context of communal monastic ritual is part of meditative development.

In scholarly religious instruction, the rote learning of long passages may be considered necessary before the student receives teaching on their meaning. The training of the memory in this manner can have impressive results: it may be possible for the student to recall the content of the text after many years. An older-generation Tibetan monk with whom I worked for some months was able to remember extensive passages of texts when needed, after perhaps forty years since his monastic college education. When he realised that a text he had studied was of relevance, he would start reciting from the beginning of the appropriate chapter or section, and once he reached the passage in question, we could then transcribe it as he repeated it. In today's world of ready access to electronic texts and internet sources the technique may seem rather redundant, but in traditional societies there may be less written sources to hand, so this kind of memory training clearly had a useful role. The development of clear recollection is also included within the Buddhist mental training of *mindfulness*. The prevalence of such memorisation in pre-modern times also helps to explain variations in the wording of citations of important scriptural sources. When Buddhist scholars wrote commentarial treatises, backing up points with scriptural quotations, they might appeal to their direct memory rather than seeking a written record of the original. Later scholars would then pick up the wording of the citation, which might have some slight re-phrasing or re-ordering, and one can trace copyings and re-copyings of the citation given without further consultation of the original text.

TEACHING AND LEARNING

Even once texts were written, oral transmission remained important for two reasons. First, oral transmission was considered an important element in teaching and learning. In part, this was related to the traditional notion that the personal relationship between the teacher and student was a basis for the transmission of the teachings. The concept of a valid lineage of transmission from master to student is built into the ideas surrounding monastic ordination. It is considered that the vows need to be received in the context of a valid ordination ceremony, from a preceptor who has himself received the vows. The existence of the texts with the lists of rules is not in itself enough. A young monk will often have a close relationship with his preceptor, whom he should respect or even venerate as the one who introduced him to his religious vocation. This notion that the master–student lineage is crucial became even more marked in tantric Buddhism as also in some East Asian traditions, particularly Chan and Zen.

In modern schools and universities, it is recognised that education is not simply a matter of an acquiring of knowledge, and the human context in which learning takes place is not dismissed even today. In traditional Asian Buddhist training, there may be less explicit recognition of a student's independent thinking – in Tibetan Buddhism, there is an image of a student as like a pot, needing to receive the liquid of the teaching poured by the teacher. But the emphasis on the ongoing two-way relationship with the teacher, and the student's own mental clarity, receptivity and purity (the pot must lack holes, it must be upright, open, and unconta-minated), means that the model of education is *in practice* one which puts much emphasis on developing the potential of the individual student. And the way that the learning environment is structured reaffirms and draws attention to the idea that the meaning of the religious teachings can only genuinely be activated through participation in the person to person transmission. A student in the Tibetan tradition normally only studies a text once it has been introduced by the teacher through a ritual transmission, performed by the teacher through a single reading, often at high speed, or sometimes integrated into teachings on the text, with the reading aloud of each passage followed by explanations of it.

ORAL TRANSMISSION AS A SUPPLEMENT TO TEXTS

Secondly, oral transmission also retained a significant place because in pre-modern Asian contexts texts were not widely distributed or read. This was especially so before the advent of printing, but even after printing was introduced, many texts were never considered important enough to print. Traditional printing methods, such as block-printing in Tibet, in any case necessitated a major investment of expertise, time and resources, with each page of writing needing to be carved out on the wooden block, after which every page of a new copy needed to be individually pressed. Even the works of famous Tibetan lamas might never be printed but simply preserved in manuscript form, apart from a few more widely circulated books and contributions to collections of writings of different lamas of the tradition. Moreover, the holy texts which were copied or printed were often produced with added embellishments or illustrations, making them even more valuable.

THE TREATMENT OF SACRED TEXTS

Books might be stored away in monastery libraries or displayed on temple altars but rarely consulted, kept more for their spiritual presence as symbolic repositories of the Dharma than for their content to be read, especially if the books were scriptures. The 'cult of the book' became especially important in Indian Mahāyāna, but everywhere in Buddhist countries, Dharma books retained a sacred character. The physical books of the Buddha's teaching were the objects of worship and offerings; they were circumambulated and prostrated to, and enshrined in *stūpa*s as well as being kept in specially constructed shelving in temples, in effect as part of the arrangement of the temple shrine. Although they were produced with great care and to very high artistic and scribal standards, religious books might remain nearly all their lives carefully wrapped in the uppermost sanctums of the temple space, from where they were thought to radiate blessings or majestic spiritual power upon the whole environment. In the Tibetan tradition, they might be taken out and ritually paraded to protect the community on special occasions, or a monastery might sponsor the reading aloud of the scriptures on a periodic basis as a meritorious religious practice and spiritual transmission. The books were therefore often hand-crafted as fitting vessels for the Buddha's presence, rather than for convenient reading. This kind of sacral book production is now being, in most cases, replaced in Asia by the more modern concept of production for reading, employing modern technologies, although contemporary Buddhist practice still includes sponsorship of high-quality text production for the purpose of generating merit.

In monastic colleges, a text might be studied very thoroughly, gone through carefully with memorisation and close analysis of each sentence. The design and layout of Tibetan Buddhist commentarial texts was especially conducive to this form of study, but not for browsing or quick reference to locate discussion of specific topics across different texts. So, recollection and oral presentation of one's learning remained important for Buddhist teachers, especially when they were teaching lay audiences who may not be literate at all.

THE SCRIPTURES WHICH ARE CONSIDERED *BUDDHA WORD*

THE EARLY SCRIPTURES AND THEIR TRANSMISSION

The earliest scriptures were the discourses (*sūtra*, Pāli *sutta*) of the Buddha or of his principal students, considered to have been inspired by the Buddha, along with the texts on the monastic rule (*vinaya*). The discourses typically begin with the phrase, 'Thus have I heard', representing a claim that they contain the words spoken by the Buddha, as witnessed and recalled by his direct disciple.

It is clear that with the earliest collection of scriptures, orally memorised and preserved, there would be questions over the authenticity of the recalled scriptures. Even with the often remarkably accurate techniques of learning and reciting, differences in versions are to be expected when transmitted down the generations in different areas. This was one of the main reasons for the creation of the different monastic schools, preserving slightly different versions of the monastic code. There is also the possibility that some texts might be lost in one area of the transmission and preserved elsewhere or, alternatively, that a new text might be introduced. We have seen in Chapter 2 that various criteria for judging the authenticity of a teaching purporting to be the Dharma are outlined in the early texts. Perhaps the most important is that the judgement should depend on whether or not the teaching agrees with the known sutta and vinaya texts. This approach reaffirms the centrality of the known corpus of scriptures, and would tend towards caution and conservatism in relation to new presentations of the teaching, although it does not close the door on the canon of scripture. Interestingly, the principle lives on and continues to be used in the assessment of new tantric revelations in the Tibetan rNying-ma system. New revelations are expected to conform to the body of tantric scriptures already in existence and, indeed, it is usual for them to incorporate large chunks of recycled text from famous tantric scriptures and liturgies.

The other perspective discussed above, that any teaching which is conducive to the reduction of the emotional afflictions and to liberation is the Dharma, allows a rather looser link with the existent teachings. This approach could rather more readily be used to justify expansion of the scriptural corpus, although it is more commonly referred to in relation to teachings which do not make claim to represent *Buddha Word* as such.

Besides variations in the number and content of the scriptural discourses and monastic texts, the first major expansion was in the recognition of the texts of Higher Teachings (*abhidharma*) as scripture by most – but not all – of the early schools. Thus, the main scriptural collection came to be referred to as the Three Baskets (*tripiṭaka*) of *vinaya*, *sūtra*, and *abhidharma*.

The abhidharma texts collected and further analysed the formulas and principles found in the earliest scriptures. They are clearly systematised presentations and not embedded within stories of the Buddha's interactions with his students. Some important early schools, such as the Sarvāstivāda, considered that later students had been inspired to compose them. The Theravāda position, however, was that they represent actual *Buddha Word*, teachings which the Buddha gave to the gods during his visit to the heavenly realms.

THE CHARACTER OF MAHĀYĀNA ADDITIONS TO THE SCRIPTURES

With the rise of the Mahāyāna, from around the first century BCE, huge quantities of further scriptures began to be generated, including the *Prajñāpāramitā (Transcendent Wisdom) Sūtras* mentioned in the chapter above. From a similar perspective to that of the Theravāda in relation to their *abhidhamma*, those who accepted the new scriptures claimed that the sūtras had actually been taught during the lifetime of the Buddha but only made known more widely later. Like the early discourses, these new sūtras generally began with the formula, 'thus have I heard'. They also include accounts of the occasion on which the Buddha or his students gave the teachings. Those teaching or said to be in the assembly of students include named advanced level bodhisattva students, often described along with associated stories of their specialisms, such as Mañjuśrī, associated with wisdom, or Samantabhadra, said to have developed vast aspirations and generosity. As we have seen in the chapters above, the world conjured up by these sūtras is often a rather visionary amazing place, as though the association with the Buddha has utterly transformed it. In fact, alongside the claim of historical authenticity, the Mahāyāna scriptures may quite frankly indicate the part of revelation in their appearance. For instance, the third chapter of one early Mahāyāna scripture, the *Pratyutpanna Samādhi Sūtra*, describes in detail the training for meeting with countless buddhas and receiving innumerable volumes of sūtras from them.

The style of these sūtras was often very different from the earlier texts. Individual sūtras might be made up of many chapters, and might include long descriptive passages and less repetition. Such sūtras or sections of them might still be memorised but the tradition was not dependent on this for its textual transmission and survival since by this time the scriptural collections were being committed to writing. In fact, Richard Gombrich, a specialist on early Buddhism, has suggested that the establishment of the Mahāyāna texts is only conceivable in a context in which scriptures have come to be written. If any similar texts had been generated earlier, they simply would not have survived, since they would not have had the support of an established group of reciters.

THE BUDDHIST TANTRAS

The tantras came to constitute a further class of Buddhist scriptures during the later era of Indian Buddhism, from around the seventh to thirteenth centuries. There is considerable overlap between the Mahāyāna sūtras and the tantras. In terms of the distinction between the two categories, the earlier (and some later) texts, which in time became classified as tantras, were often entitled sūtras. In terms of content, Mahāyāna sūtras often contained strings of sacred syllables, generally called *dhāraṇīs*, to be recited for meditative or protective purposes. Short texts of such *dhāraṇīs*, often associated with praises and invocation of a particular deity, began to appear from around the third century CE. In Northern Buddhist textual collections, some such texts are classified with Mahāyāna sūtras while others are classified as lower tantras.

We find texts more clearly conceptualising the use of tantric techniques as a path to Enlightenment from about the seventh century CE. These texts were presented as *Buddha Word*, with the sūtra style opening phrase, 'thus have I heard', and variations on the sūtra framing narratives of the Buddha – often, a Buddha residing in a Buddha field of wondrous qualities, teaching an assembly of advanced bodhisattvas. These tantric scriptures tend to present themselves as esoteric instructions for ritual meditations to transform everyday reality into an enlightened display, a *maṇḍala* of buddha emanations, using physical gestures and yoga, the recitation of *mantra* sacred syllables, visualisation and mental disciplines, and a strict code of conduct binding the initiate to the specific practice and its associated community. The earlier period of such tantras in India from the seventh century produced texts such as the *Mahāvairocana Tantra*, which became the basis for esoteric Buddhism in East Asia and which were also important in the early period in which Buddhism was established in Tibet. In the final centuries until Buddhism disappeared in India around the thirteenth century, tantric production continued to flourish, and with each wave of movement of Buddhism to Tibet until its demise in India, further tantras were imported, resulting in huge numbers of the Tibetan translations of tantras.

BUDDHIST TEXTUAL PRESERVATION AND DEVELOPMENT

TEXTUAL SPECIALISM

By the early centuries of the Christian era, Buddhist scriptures were being written down and copied by monk scribes trained for the purpose and new texts were being composed to add to them. The Pāli literature and that of the other early schools also expanded, as commentaries and supplementary texts were added to the corpus. Buddhist scriptures come on a vastly bigger scale than Christian scripture. Moreover, although there were some sections, such as the list of monastic rules, which were well known throughout Buddhist monasteries in different areas, there had also been significant specialisation in particular parts of the corpus from the outset, with reciters becoming expert in one group of texts. In Mahāyāna Buddhism, cults developed around individual sūtras, and this became especially pronounced in East Asian Buddhism where new Buddhist schools were formed based on specific Mahāyāna sūtras. In particular, schools arose devoted to the *Lotus Sūtra (Saddharmapuṇḍarīka)*, the *Avataṃsaka Sūtra* and the *Sukhāvatīvyūha Sūtra*s. Nothing quite parallel happened in Northern Buddhism, where the major schools retained a broad curriculum, but nonetheless, specialisms in particular scriptures were important, although in this case, the specialism generally related to the favoured tantric tradition. Perhaps it is unsurprising that the East Asian cases where there was an exclusive focus on one Mahāyāna Sūtra – and especially on the relatively short *Sukhāvatīvyūha* and *Lotus Sūtra*s – are precisely those cases where lay groups became central. It is in the more monastic traditions, with their developing schools of scholarship and learning, that we find the impetus to preserve the full heritage of Buddhist scriptures.

TRANSMISSION OF THE SCRIPTURES IN THE DIFFERENT TRADITIONS

It was monastics who had the task of first memorising and later preserving the texts in written form. Buddhist texts were virtually all compiled or composed by monks, and certainly preserved and edited by monks, mostly for a readership – or users – who were monks or nuns. Sri Lankan monk scholars compiled and edited the texts of the Pāli Canon, and added their own commentarial writings to the Theravāda textual corpus. Pāli was retained as the sacred language of the scriptures, so that the study of Pāli continued amongst a scholarly elite of monks, and the liturgical chanting of Pāli is widespread throughout different Southern Buddhist countries. Pāli was, however, transcribed into different local scripts, such as Sinhala, Khmer, and Burmese, so 'Pāli texts' do not have a uniform appearance. In the nineteenth century, Pāli scriptures were also transliterated into Roman script.

In Northern and East Asian Buddhism, the translation of scriptures was a major project, taking place over hundreds of years. Unlike the preservation of the Theravāda corpus in Pāli, translation teams worked on rendering Sanskrit early sūtra, vinaya and abhidharma, Mahāyāna sūtra and tantric works into Chinese and Tibetan. In many cases, a translation would be revised later, or an entirely new translation made, perhaps from a text which had in the meantime expanded or changed within India. Moreover, there was not always a simple transmission from Indian Sanskrit sources into Chinese or Tibetan. Some translations were made from Central Asian languages. Buddhism travelled to China along the Asian Silk route, and, before the Islamic expansion, areas to the north-west of India and the Central Asian city states had significant Buddhist presence. There was Central Asian input into Buddhist expansion into China in the early centuries of the Christian Era and also into Tibet when the Tibetan empire expanded into Central Asia between the seventh to ninth centuries.

A further complication is that in India the scriptural collection had never been closed, and an almost standard template for revelations of scriptures had developed. This culture of creativity no doubt also travelled with Buddhism. It seems that Chinese Buddhist scriptures accepted into the later canon of translated scriptures from Sanskrit works composed or compiled first in China in the early centuries CE in China. Modern scholars have even suggested that some Chinese apocryphal scriptures were translated from Chinese to Sanskrit, so that texts long assumed to have been composed first in Sanskrit may not have been Indian at all.

The translations of scriptures required team work and major sponsorship, so generally, there was involvement of political authorities in the areas concerned. When Buddhism was first introduced into Tibet, translation work was done under Imperial auspices, and in the late eighth to early ninth century, spellings and technical terms used as equivalents for Buddhist Sanskrit terms were standardised. Translations of Buddhist texts were revised in accordance with the new system. Although later translations were done after the collapse of the Empire, the usefulness of the standardised equivalents continued to be recognised. The rigidity of a rather slavish adherence to fixed sets of equivalents for Buddhist terms means that sometimes Buddhist scriptural texts in Tibetan may seem dry and scholastic, and only make any sense at all when we understand the full implications of the technical terms. But for modern scholars, the fact that Tibetan translations are often very close to their Sanskrit originals means that they may sometimes be rather more useful for reconstructing earlier Indian Buddhist materials than, for instance, the rather freer Chinese Buddhist translations of the same texts, or of earlier versions of them.

Printing was invented in China and the reproduction of Buddhist texts was one of its early applications. The first dated printed book is the Mahāyāna *Diamond Sūtra* in Chinese, dated to 868 CE, although the block-printing technique had been in use for more than a century before. Clearly, printing implied a greater circulation for Buddhist scriptures, although block-printing still required considerable investment, and the sponsorship of beautiful manuscript texts also continued as meritorious work. Movable type was not well suited to traditional Chinese script, so it did not fully supplant block-printing after its invention in the thirteenth century.

The major scriptural collections were generally compiled under State sponsorship. The first complete woodblock edition of the Chinese Buddhist canon was produced during the Song Dynasty in the tenth century, on over 5,000 scrolls. In the thirteenth century, an important edition of the Chinese canon was produced, and this was no doubt a significant model for Tibetans in making their textual collections in an era when both the Chinese and Tibetans came under the Mongol Yuan dynasty. One important influence was the notion of Indian origin as guaranteeing the authenticity of a doubtful text. The Chinese collections, however, retained texts which had much earlier entered the accepted corpus of scriptures. In Tibet, the rigorous criteria applied from their first canon-making in the early fourteenth century of not accepting texts lacking

Sanskrit originals meant that a large stock of tantric scriptures was excluded. A further collection of tantric scriptures, some of which derived from the early translation period and some of which were compiled or composed in Tibet, was later made by the followers of the early traditions. Editorial work on the different collections resulted in a number of versions of Tibetan Buddhist canonical collections, as well as related collections of commentarial works. Tibetan scriptures were later translated into Mongolian, as Tibetan forms of Buddhism expanded northwards.

Many versions of the Chinese Buddhist canon were produced after the first in the tenth century. Additions to the corpus were carefully controlled, although each edition had large numbers of texts since it would contain different versions of similar material, such as different early translations from different times of many of the sūtras, and the vinaya texts of more than one school. The most widely used edition now is the Japanese Taishō edition produced in the 1920s. It has fifty-five volumes, based ultimately on a thirteenth-century Korean woodblock edition, and a further forty-five volumes of Japanese Buddhist texts and illustrations.

CHAPTER SUMMARY

- The *Buddha Word* or scripture is considered to stand in for the Buddha.
- In the early period, the scriptures were preserved orally, which affects their content.
- Oral transmission has also been important in traditional learning.
- Sacred scriptures may be worshipped as much as read.
- Expansion of the scriptures was allowed under certain circumstances.
- The *abhidharma* (Higher Teachings) was added to the sūtra and vinaya texts, forming the 'Three Baskets' (*tripiṭaka*).
- The Mahāyāna tradition added many more sūtras and later tantras to the textual corpus; some East Asian schools have focused on a particular sūtra.
- Theravāda Buddhism retained Pāli as a sacred language but transcribed it in different scripts.
- Other Buddhist traditions translated the sacred texts, over long periods of time, often with the help of the political authorities of the area, and later, various canonical collections of scriptures were made.

FURTHER READING

Gombrich, Richard 1990 'How the Mahāyāna Began'. An article particularly interesting for its discussion of the role of writing in Mahāyāna beginnings.

Rewata Dhamma, U and Bhikkhu, Bodhi 'Introduction' to *A Comprehensive Manual of Abhidhamma*. www.accesstoinsight.org/lib/authors/bodhi/abhiman. html. A short introduction to the Theravāda Abhidhamma.

SCRIPTURAL SOURCES

There are so many Buddhist scriptures, the following are necessarily a narrow selection.

THERAVĀDA THREE BASKETS

Bullitt, John 2009 *Access to Insight: Readings in Theravada Buddhism*. www.access toinsight.org/. Specifically: www.accesstoinsight.org/tipitaka/index.html *The Tipitaka*. www.metta.lk/tipitaka/

MAHĀYĀNA SŪTRAS

The *Pratyutpanna Samādhi Sūtra*, translated by Lokakṣema, and translated from the Chinese by Paul Harrison, 1998, pp. 1–116. A Mahāyāna sūtra with a description in Chapter 3 of methods for encountering the Buddhas of the present.

The *Saddharmapuṇḍarīka* (*Lotus Sūtra*), www.sacred-texts.com/bud/lotus/index. htm. An old translation; there are numerous more recent translations with commentaries, but this worthy classic is available on the internet.

Cleary, Thomas (translated from Chinese) 1987 *The Flower Ornament Scripture. The Avatamsaka Sutra*.

Conze, Edward 1973 *The Perfection of Wisdom in Eight Thousand Lines and its Verse Summary*.

Lamotte, Étienne 1976 *The Teaching of Vimalakīrti (Vimalakīrtinirdeśa)*.

BUDDHIST TANTRAS

The root tantras are generally fairly impenetrable without extensive introduction, but the two examples here should give some indication of the approach.

Davidson, Ronald M. 1995 "The Litany of Names of Mañjuśrī", in Donald S. Lopez (ed.) *Religions of India in Practice*, Princeton: Princeton University Press, pp. 104–25.

Hodge, S. (trans.) 2003 *The Mahā-Vairocana-Abhisaṃbodhi Tantra with Buddhaguhya's Commentary*. Translation of an early Buddhist tantra which had a major impact on East Asian as well as Northern Buddhism.

4

THE SANGHA

WHERE DO MONASTICS FIT?

We have seen in Chapter 2 that Buddhist monastics are not expected to intervene in many areas of secular life. The householder/monk opposition is most clearly expressed in the *vinaya* rules relating to livelihood. Monks are prohibited from any remunerative employment or work by which their basic subsistence could directly be produced, including agricultural tasks, trade, medical or astrological work, and so on. The clear practical implication of this is that, by definition, the monastic community is dependent upon lay support. This theoretical ideal for the operation of monastic/lay relations was historically often modified in various ways, especially in the case of large-scale wealthy and powerful monastic institutions, which developed in different parts of pre-modern Asia. But in principle, and often in practice from the perspective of individual monks, monastics must receive their basic necessities from the lay community. They are a respected group representing spiritual values, set apart but connected to the laity in a relationship of mutual dependency and support. Where the full code is maintained intact, the only alternative to dependence on lay people is an ascetic life, entailing distance from human communities, surviving, for example, by wearing discarded rags and subsisting on foraged or discarded foods requiring no digging or work effort. The Buddha himself had emerged from the ranks of the ancient Indian wandering ascetic movement, and its uncompromising ascetic and non-worldly code left its mark on the Buddhist monastic rule, most clearly in the preservation of the *four resorts*. These are alms for food, discarded rags for clothing, a tree for shelter, and fermented cattle urine for medicine, and they are symbolically acknowledged in the monk's ordination ceremony. Yet the early Buddhist monastic code toned down this discipline in line with the Middle Way principle of avoiding the extremes of indulgence or asceticism, and more ascetic practices remained simply as options for a minority. The mainstream Buddhist model for the religious life rather became that of the monk who is removed from the worldly involvements of householders, unlike the household brahman priest, yet who may remain close to the lay community, in contrast to the forest-dwelling naked Jain ascetic. Eating moderately the food given to him, wearing basic and unadorned robes, the Buddhist monk should act with decorum, demonstrate upright morality and, in dealings with the laity, represent the values of the contemplative life.

MONASTIC AND OTHER RELIGIOUS ROLES

More specifically, what are monks expected to do? The third of the Jewels in which Refuge is taken is the Noble or Holy Sangha, the Buddhist Order or community who have attained at least the lesser spiritual levels of sanctity which are irreversible, guaranteeing eventual Enlightenment. In Mahāyāna Buddhist contexts, bodhisattvas established in the bodhisattva spiritual levels, similarly considered irreversible stages, are also included. It is through the Noble Sangha that the Buddha and the Dharma can be accessed. This group, capable of inspiring and leading others on the Noble Path, are a fitting and worthy 'field' in which to plant seeds of virtuous deeds, later to grow and ripen into good circumstances and spiritual understanding. In the accounts given in the early scriptures, it is clear that many of the early disciples had attained the levels of sanctity. Indeed, the first Communal Recitation of the collected scriptures after the Buddha passed away was supposed to have involved five hundred *arhat*s or Enlightened ones. In such an environment, it is hardly surprising that the notion of the Noble

Sangha, and that of the larger order, including the ordinary unenlightened monks and nuns, would merge into each other in references to the Sangha. In any case, the Sangha as a whole became the Buddha's representatives, all the more so perhaps once he had passed away, apparently deliberately avoiding the naming of a single individual as a successor or leader of the movement, at least according to the Pāli tradition.

Put simply, monastics have the job of representing the Buddha and seeking, ideally and as far as possible, to approximate to an embodiment of the Noble Sangha. Their work, then, is not only to help themselves in their individual spiritual paths but to provide the means for others to progress. In fact, although Buddhism puts great stress on individuals taking personal responsibility and striving for realisation, it also has an important communal dimension. As well as matters pertaining to the training of the monk's mind and emotions, the Buddhist monastic rules concern relations within the monastic community and relations with the laity. As we have seen, venerating and making offerings to monastics are central features of lay Buddhist practice in Asia. Even without any specific activity apart from graceful acceptance of the offering, the Order of monks gives lay people the chance to generate merit. Cynics might suggest that it sounds like a convenient ideology to justify monks' privilege, but it is worth reflecting that the social practice creates lay people as active participants in the religious exchange in a way which may bring benefits beyond the future metaphysical rewards, including considerable leverage over the monastic community. The South-east Asian example of an entire family, and especially the mother, being considered to gain much merit – and an element of social prestige – through offering a young son to ordain as a monk for a period demonstrates that it is not always the monk recipients who are principally in control of the relationship.

THE MONASTIC DISCIPLINE

In what other ways do monks represent the Master? The main and most obvious task for the monk is to uphold the monastic discipline. The essentials of the monastic or *vinaya* code quite possibly derive from the Buddha himself and the first generations of Buddhists. Later, as the early Buddhist schools separated from each other, they maintained their own sets of monastic precepts, but it is remarkable how similar the different versions remained. It therefore seems likely that the core of the discipline goes back to the ancient period before the Buddhist movement split into discrete orders. An alternative interpretation is that agreement across the different schools on the contrary indicates later conflated materials, since the archaeological sources suggest the orders only became entirely separate around the second century CE. Even in this case, such agreement would then at the least represent a clear ideological position on which the early Buddhist tradition could agree. The regular gathering to confess infractions and to reaffirm the monastic precepts in a communal recitation is generally the most important monastic ritual, defining each monastic community, as well as constituting the expression of the Buddhist monastic ethos. The importance of the rules is not simply that they serve as a useful condition for the religious life. It is not merely that the monks' lifestyle provides the most suitable opportunities for serious religious practice, although it is considered to do this by relieving the aspirant from the duties and worries of the householder. More than this, we have seen in Chapter 2 that the discipline *in itself* constitutes an expression of the spiritual path. The rules nurture the habit of unsullied upright behaviour and, just as importantly, the habit of mindful awareness, since the numerous points need to be readily recalled and applied to one's mental states, bodily actions and speech. Moreover, they embody the principles of the Middle Way between indulgence and asceticism.

THE MIDDLE WAY IN THE MONASTIC CODE

A good example of the Middle Way principle is the rules on food, which have already been mentioned in Chapter 2 in relation to meat eating. The code forbids both over-eating and starving oneself. In accepting offerings, the monk should not discriminate between desirable and undesirable foods, yet there is the duty to check that the foods given have not been procured through harming living beings. Apart from those opting to adopt a stricter regime, the Buddhist monastic rule did not involve a rigorous dietary discipline such as that followed by Jain ascetics. The example shows clearly the Middle Way approach both in terms of the individual ethical practice and also in terms of the character of the Buddhist Order in its relations with the laity, representing a disciplined and ethically upright group and of good reputation as a religious community, thus worthy of lay respect but not so distant from lay life that excessive expectations would create a burden.

Similarly, in the case of clothing, ascetic nakedness was avoided from the start, and the earlier ascetic discarded rags were replaced (for the majority – they could be retained if wanted) by a practical and distinctive uniform, robes dyed in a single colour, of sewn together pieces of material which could be donated by lay people, and ensure the smart appearance and decorum of Buddhist monks. Yet no more than one set of three robes should be owned, and nor should further decorative embellishments be added.

THE RULE AS THE PATH: BEYOND MONASTICISM

The early Buddhist approach that the Sangha's discipline in itself expresses the religious life has been resilient, not only in the continued survival of the monastic code itself but also in important strands of later Buddhist doctrine and practice. In particular, the bodhisattva path similarly came to be structured on the basis of sets of bodhisattva rules of training, which again in some sense embody the ethos of the spiritual path. In this case, the specific precepts are associated with one or another of the bodhisattva transcendent actions. Perhaps even more strikingly, the Buddhist Mantra Vehicle teachings made the equivalent tantric code of conduct – the samaya rules – so central that there is an oft-repeated maxim that merely to preserve the samaya discipline is sufficient for Enlightenment to be attained in the end, despite neglecting to perform any other practice. Moreover, this tantric ethic, like the monastic code, not only relates to individual spiritual discipline, but also to the coherence of the tantric community, relations within it and relations with outsiders, in an attempt to focus on and live out the enlightened vision within everyday social relationships. And the main communal tantric ritual gathering, which all practitioners are expected to participate in at least twice a month, involves at its core confession and purification of transgressions of the samaya discipline. In Tibetan monasteries, this ritual in some senses may supersede the regular reaffirmation of the monks' code as the central repeated rite, and may attract the participation of unaffiliated or part-time tantric practitioners in the community.

THE ULTIMATE DISCIPLINE

In the advanced Tibetan meditative traditions, some teachers suggest that instead of focusing on the many individual rules the tantric discipline can be kept to by 'dwelling in the nature of mind'. Similarly, the Thai meditation master Ajahn Chah comments on the monastic code: 'The scriptures tell us that we must examine ourselves regarding each and every rule and keep them all strictly ... Some teachers teach in this manner ... It just can't work that way'. A footnote adds: 'On another occasion the Venerable Ajahn completed the analogy by saying that if we know how to guard our own minds, then it is the same as observing all the numerous rules of the Vinaya' (Ven. Ajahn Chah 1982 *Bodhinyāna*, Bung Wai Forest Monastery 85–86).

MONKS' DUTIES BEYOND THE DISCIPLINE

Beyond the preservation of the discipline as such, how else should monks approximate to the Noble Sangha? In the Theravāda tradition, a notion of two kinds of vocations for monks came about, a division which summarises well the two principal tasks for the Sangha and the two slightly different specialisms which have run through the larger Buddhist fold. The vocation of *insight duty* (*vipassanā-dhura*) is concerned with developing the meditative practice of the spiritual path, keeping alive the possibility of the attainment of Enlightenment. The vocation of *book duty* (*gantha-dhura*), on the other hand, involves all the tasks needed to preserve the teachings about the spiritual path, including textual work to ensure the transmission of the scriptures, scholarship to ensure that intellectual understanding of the tradition is maintained, teaching to pass on and to spread the principles and practice of the path. We will have more to say about the lifestyles and approaches of the virtuoso Buddhist hermits and forest meditators. The majority of monks, however, have resided in town or village monasteries, and many would have been more inclined to identify with the duty of study and teaching. The dedicated scholars were also generally a relatively small group. But a slightly different way of expressing the distinction changes the emphasis a little. On one hand there are those focused on intensive training in internal meditative states to gain realisation, while others give their energies to spread and promote the Buddhist teachings and practice in the wider world.

THE INJUNCTION TO TEACH

Famously, the Buddha was said to have charged his then few disciples with universal communication of the message:

> Go forth for the good of the many, for the happiness of the many, out of compassion for the world, for the welfare, the good and the happiness of gods and men. Let no two of you go in the same direction. Teach the Dharma which is beautiful in the beginning, beautiful in the middle and beautiful at the end.
>
> (Vin I.20, *The Buddha and His Disciples*, www.buddhanet.net/ e-learning/buddhism/disciples06.htm; also found at SN 4.5).

The ultimate success of the Buddhist tradition in Asia has much to do with continued attention to both sides of the coin: serious practitioners were able to keep alive meditative and insight practice traditions associated with the Buddha's Enlightenment, while effective establishment and social organisation of Buddhist institutions enabled the preservation, continuity and development of the teachings and practice. This involved the production and maintenance of a vast corpus of scriptural and commentarial literature, as well as a rich range of cultural artefacts encoding other important symbolic elements of Buddhist transmission − *stūpa*s, temples, Buddha images, artistic and dramatic expressions of Buddhist teaching. It also depended upon ongoing engagement between the Buddhist monastic community and the wider societies in which they lived.

To a greater or lesser extent, 'ordinary' monastics who might neither be trained in the more technical meditative techniques usually developed in retreat nor highly learned in the niceties of Buddhist philosophy have contributed to such engagement. Furthermore, while it is worth distinguishing between elite practitioners, scholars, or renowned Buddhist teachers, and more ordinary monks and nuns, it is also worth remembering that there need not be any great gulf between the groups concerned. Famous monk exemplars may have direct involvements in monasteries under their direction and the specialists may have earlier direct experience of teaching and practice in ordinary monasteries (much of which they might integrate into their more advanced training), not to mention lay Buddhist traditions they learnt in childhood.

Specific activities that monks across the Asian Buddhist world might perform include direct Buddhist teaching of more junior monastics and of lay people, and monastic ritual practices of various kinds, both as part of regular or seasonal acts of religious devotion or contemplation and as services for lay people.

The teaching of the lay community is often tied into the ritualised set of exchanges between monks and laity, such as occasions when the lay community publicly provides food and other support for the monks in Southern Buddhist countries, or at the culminating festival of a lay sponsored monastic practice of a tantric ritual cycle in Northern Buddhist contexts. Monks may also be invited to teach as part of community or family events.

We have seen in Chapter 2 that as part of the broad category of training in Meditative Absorption, monks may perform a variety of ritual and meditative practices, some focused on their own development or on the monastic community and others as services for lay sponsors. In Southern Buddhist contexts, monks may recite *paritta*s, protective Pāli verses or suttas, to guard against harm or to engender health or well-being for lay people. In Northern Buddhism, tantric rituals are generally used for similar purposes. One important classification of tantric practice divides it into the main practice which achieves Enlightenment and the subsidiary practices dependent on prior performance of the main practice. These subsidiaries are designed to destroy evil influences and they may be performed during a public festival at the end of the Tibetan year, thought to expel the community's stock of harmful influences which have accumulated over the year. Asian Buddhist societies also have non-monastic folk ritualists who perform rituals for lay people, often for self-seeking purposes which may not be considered seemly for monastic involvement. In Northern Buddhist contexts, however, the Buddhist religious system tends to monopolise a greater proportion of ritual services than in Southern Buddhism, tantric texts often engaging with more frankly 'worldly' motives, yet integrating them with exalted aims of universal benefit and wisdom.

East Asian environments provide a slightly different case. There may be a clear division of labour between different religious roles, people often having simultaneous affiliation to more than one religion. In Japan, for example, counts of followers of different religions generally end up with figures much higher than the total population. Confucianism was strongly rooted in China before Buddhism arrived and remained central to community life until recent times. Buddhism and Daoism also left a legacy in the region. So different ritual specialists may be called upon for different purposes and, in this environment, Buddhist monks or priests may become associated with a particular specialism, such as funerary and memorial rites in Japan. In fact, different groups of Buddhists may be associated with rather different specialisms, as we see in a fourteenth-century Ming Emperor's public statement about the harmonious roles of different religious traditions (Stephan Feuchtwang 2001: 170). This document sees Chan as intended for the cultivation of the individual, while other Buddhist practices, possibly those based on the *White Lotus Sūtra*, are considered to be more involved in family and social relations. On the other hand, there was also greater syncretism between Buddhism and indigenous traditions in East Asia, so again in the case of the Japanese example, the Buddhist rites incorporate a good deal of ritual and symbolic elements concerning ancestors which originally stem from Confucian and Japanese traditions of ancestor veneration.

NON-MONASTIC SPECIALISTS: BUDDHIST PRIESTS AND BUDDHIST MANTRA PRACTITIONERS

In Southern Buddhism, the monkhood has been virtually synonymous with full-time Buddhist commitment. There are some examples of lay roles overlapping with monks' duties, such as specialist laymen chanters in Thailand, who the authorities tried and failed to ban. Temporary ordination of young men in South-east Asia also meant that knowledge of Buddhist practice was widespread amongst the populace. But generally, non-monastic ritual specialists were rarely considered to have any particular Buddhist expertise. To some extent, the picture has been modified by the contemporary development of lay Buddhist organisations in urban areas. But in East Asian and Northern Buddhism, there were more non-monastic alternatives for serious religious practice, often based on Mahāyāna models for lay practitioners.

In the case of Tibetan Buddhism, the hereditary principle for transmission and training in tantric Buddhist lineages became widespread in the post-Imperial period (ninth to eleventh centuries) after the collapse of large-scale State patronage of Buddhist institutions. This style of early Tibetan Buddhist family lineages left a legacy on both elite Buddhist practice and also on local communities. Many of the eventual large-scale monasteries had high-status lamas with hereditary lineages as well as monk lamas, and there were close connections between the major religious families and the monasteries. Hereditary lamas or in some cases self-made non-monastic lamas might also have a part in local communities, performing Buddhist practices in a part-time or full-time capacity, often administering to lay needs such as weather control and protective rites. In parts, whole villages or settlements of such ritual specialists and their families grew up: the term, 'yellow householders' was used, expressing the mixed monk/lay status. Specialists in tantric ritual, *mantra practitioners* (*sngags pa*), ideally and often in practice may have received intensive training comparable to that in a monastery, with at least a three-year retreat and much practice of the specific tantra cycles in which the lama or his tradition specialises. Where the lineage is hereditary, a good deal of training would take place in childhood, with the father or paternal uncle teaching the boy and, in the case of communities of 'yellow householders', there would be even more everyday support for developing a life around Buddhist ritual practice. A *mantra practitioner* would be expected to maintain his own regular tantric practice as well as performing rituals for the community. A more reclusive *mantra practitioner* who may avoid commitments to a specific community might become close or merge into a third category of religious specialists in Northern Buddhism: that of the hermit yogin, often – though not always – non-monastic, practising Buddhist meditation in retreat conditions as a way of life, sometimes for several decades.

In East Asian Buddhism, especially where the State did not support the Buddhist monastic Sangha, non-monastic religious specialists have often been central to the transmission and preservation of the tradition. Although Buddhist monasteries were often part of the socioeconomic fabric of society in China, they had variable relations with the State, which was at times hostile. Under such circumstances, it is not surprising that some resilient forms of Chinese and East Asian Buddhism have been less dependent on traditional Buddhist monastic organisation. For instance, early Chinese Buddhist monasteries allowed some relaxation of the vinaya rule which prevented monks from productive work. Such traditions became associated with the Chinese Chan lineage, especially in the Japanese tradition of Chan (Japanese: Zen), and a discipline developed in which manual labour could be treated as part of the spiritual training. Thus, there was less need for complete dependency on the laity.

A different kind of alternative is represented by Buddhist movements in which lay people fully participated, the practices made less technical and more simple and accessible. Thus, the Pure Land School (*Jingtu* = Japanese *Jōdo*), founded in the early fifth century, focused on worship of the Buddha Amitābha. It successfully became established in Japan (twelfth–thirteenth centuries), where an offshoot, the True Pure Land School, eventually became the largest, but not only, group among Pure Land followers. Their emphasis on *other-power* (see Chapter 2) implied a doctrinal as well as practical shift from monasticism. Lay priests provide services such as leading memorials and funerals. Similar trends to simple practice which can be perfected by lay people are also features of other Japanese Buddhist schools, for instance those basing themselves on the *Lotus Sūtra*. As a contemporary example, the Sōka Gakkai is a modern offshoot from the thirteenth-century Nichiren movement, and it is based on an international lay association. But in Japan too, monasticism had its periods of strength when it received political patronage. Rinzai Zen monasteries had a privileged relationship with the State in the fifteenth century. In the Edo or Tokugawa period (seventeenth–late nineteenth centuries), officially sanctioned forms of Buddhism were integrated into the State social structure, but in a carefully controlled manner. After the Meiji Restoration in 1868, in the opening years of the new regime, Buddhist elements were removed from contexts involving Shintō, Japanese rites which became the State religion. Buddhist monks and nuns were encouraged to disrobe and Buddhist temples which had previously been presided over by monks came to be looked after by hereditary priests as celibacy was no longer required for Buddhist clerics. So it is worth remembering that the domination of non-monastics in contemporary Japanese Buddhism is not altogether characteristic of Japanese Buddhism historically. At the same time, East Asian Buddhist traditions went much further than Northern and Southern Buddhism in developing lay-controlled Buddhist practice.

MONASTERIES AND SOCIETY

THE MONK/LAY OPPOSITION

Throughout Buddhist history in much of Asia, monasteries have been the mainstay of Buddhism. As we have seen, the monastic Sangha, preserving the Dharma and acting as the pivotal point for Buddhist practice, became the main symbol of the Noble Sangha Refuge. Monastic life was mostly considered virtually indispensable to serious spiritual practice. The early texts record some cases of lay people becoming enlightened but it was generally felt the Middle Way is best practised by *going forth* from the household life. The main role for householders in early times and in many later contexts is to support the Sangha and to practise moral discipline, thus storing up great merit which would come to fruition in future lives. Teachings on meditation and wisdom were mostly reserved for monks.

In the early Mahāyāna, there was some explicit challenge to this kind of dualistic opposition between the categories of householder and monk. The *Vimalakīrtinirdeśasūtra*'s teaching is based on its account of the householder, Vimalakīrti, who demonstrates greater spiritual accomplishment and wisdom than any of the other disciples of the Buddha, including the Buddha's famous personal students of the early texts and the principal bodhisattva students. The *Vimalakīrtinirdeśasūtra* recounts a series of incidents designed to illustrate that ultimately the categories of monk and lay, male and female, have no valid significance. Similar sentiments are found occasionally in earlier sources. The Pāli accounts of enlightened nuns of the Buddha's time and the equivalent texts preserved in the Chinese collections contain reflections on the irrelevance of male and female characteristics for the spiritual path, although they do not express such an explicit challenge to the male-dominated order of monks. This teaching is only in fact felt forcefully because the Buddhist Sangha was so firmly based on the principles of stratification on the grounds of monastic and gender status. Moreover, archaeological sources would seem to show that such conventional categories were if anything hardened and made more inflexible under Gupta rule in northern India (280–550) at the very time the Mahāyāna teachings were developing along with a resurgent Hinduism. Paradoxically, then, such explicit teachings may reflect rigidity in everyday social structure rather than the reverse.

THE *VIMALAKĪRTINIRDEŚASŪTRA*

Extract from Chapter 6. Mahāyāna sūtras often embed their teachings in dramatic stories of the Buddha and his students. The context for this extract is that a goddess (Sanskrit, *devī*) has joined the group listening to the teachings of Vimalakīrti, the layman, and she has stunned the audience with her wisdom and eloquence, successfully sparring with Śāriputra, one of the principal students of the Buddha who was famed in early Buddhism as the ideal monk, foremost in wisdom. Śāriputra, unwilling to be bested by a female, challenges the goddess to change her womanhood. If she does so, it demonstrates that she is not really female at all, but if she fails to do so, it would seem to highlight her gender inferiority. Here is her response:

Devī: For ... years ... I have sought after womanhood, without ever obtaining it. How then could I change it? Honourable Śāriputra, if a skilful illusionist created through transformation an illusionary woman, could you reasonably ask her why she does not change her womanhood?

Śāriputra – Certainly not, O Devī, every illusionary creation being unreal, how could it be changed?

Devī – Equally, Honourable Śāriputra, all dharmas [*i.e. phenomena*] are unreal and of a nature created by illusion, and you would think of asking them to change their womanhood?

Then the Devī carried out such a supernatural action that Śāriputra the Elder appeared in every way like the Devī and she herself appeared in every way like Śāriputra the Elder.

Then the Devī changed into Śāriputra asked Śāriputra changed into a goddess: Why then, O Honourable Sir, do you not change your womanhood?

> Śāriputra changed into a goddess replied: I do not know either how I
>   lost my masculine form, or how I acquired a feminine body.
> The Devī replied: If, O Elder, you were capable of changing a feminine
>   form, then all women could change their womanhood. Just as, O
>   Elder, you appear a woman, so also all women appear in the form
>   of a woman, but it is without being women that they appear in the
>   form of women.
> It is with this hidden intention that the Blessed One [*i.e. the Buddha*]
> has said: Dharmas [*i.e. phenomena*] are neither male nor female.
>   (E. Lamotte 1976 *The Teaching of Vimalakīrti*: 170–71)

MONASTIC INSTITUTIONS WITHIN SOCIETY

Throughout the history of Buddhism in India, the religion essentially
remained based in monasteries, even though there were some non-
monastic wanderers or hermits as well as some scope for lay involvements and, in the later period, some tantric gurus who might
have infringed all the usual definitions of religious exemplars. Thus,
the fortunes of the Buddhist tradition are intertwined with the
health of the monastic institutions and their abilities to interrelate
with lay populations.

One disadvantage of the tradition's dependency on the monastic
order is that it is easier for the tradition to be seriously weakened or
wiped out altogether in difficult times. Monasteries make easy
targets for invaders and this was a major factor in the demise of
Buddhism in India in the early centuries of the second millennium of
the Christian era. Indirectly, also, political upheavals can impact on
monasteries when the lay sponsors are hard-pressed and unable to provide support. Agricultural or economic problems can also mean the end
of funding. In Sri Lanka, Buddhism was almost destroyed on a number
of occasions, and it seems that the scriptures were first committed to
writing after a famine in which the schools of reciters who specialised in
memorising different portions of the Canon were decimated.

On the other hand, in prosperous periods, the system allowed for
a high level of cultural and educational achievement, and the
dependency of monks on the laity meant that the relationship was
not altogether unequal despite the difference in spiritual status
between monks and lay people. There is, for instance, a rule that

monks and nuns are not allowed to refuse a request to teach. In this way, Buddhism distanced itself from the exclusiveness of Brahmanism. The principle was generally applied also to other invitations, for ritual services and so on. The ideal of harmonious relations between the monastic and lay communities is eulogised in many Buddhist sources. In Tibetan Buddhism, there is the idea that the expert meditators are so connected up with their patrons in a single tantric circle or *maṇḍala* that they will eventually attain realisation together.

THE INTERDEPENDENCY OF THE PROFESSIONAL RELIGIOUS AND THEIR PATRONS 1

The Tibetan culture hero and poet saint, Mi-la-ras-pa (circa 1052–1135) is attributed with teaching:

> Between the hermit meditating in the mountains
> and the donor who provides his sustenance
> There is a link that will lead them to Enlightenment together.
>
> (Patrul Rinpoche 1994: 327)

Beyond the ideology, community involvement may often contribute to a local monastery becoming a source of a local group's identity and pride. The monastery and its monks may serve to represent the community's symbolic values and aspirations, while also playing a part in the local social dynamics, the monks being recruited from families in the area. Thus, after the Chinese invasion of Tibet in the mid-twentieth century, there were instances of solidarity between monastics and lay people in seeking to preserve monasteries, such as cases where a local group left and worked together over many years to rebuild their monastery in exile in India. The community dimension to Buddhist monastic practice is not fully recognised in official Chinese Government sources, claiming to guarantee the freedom of belief and private religious devotions. But the essence of religious practice for Tibetans may just as importantly entail community work on and direct sponsorship of the local monastery. Rules governing the funding and operation of monasteries, in which Government bodies oversee monastic activities and channel payments, may create problems for this traditional relationship.

THE INTERDEPENDENCY OF THE PROFESSIONAL RELIGIOUS AND THEIR PATRONS 2

The restoration of the monasteries is very much a collective project through which Tibetans aim to recover the principal traditional means of acquiring religious merit ... The relationship of lay people to monks is expressed in traditional Buddhist terms as the relationship of patrons and benefactors (*sbyin bdag*) to an institution which embodies the highest spiritual values of Tibetan society. Yet this is precisely the relationship that Chinese religious policy finds politically threatening.

(Ronald Schwartz 1994 'Buddhism, nationalist protest and the state in Tibet': 731)

THE PRINCIPLES OF BUDDHIST MONASTIC ORGANISATION

The organisational principles of the monastic order, as embodied in the vinaya and early sutta texts, are in important respects egalitarian and non-hierarchical, and based on small-scale organisational units. They are likely to go back to the Buddha's own lifetime, and are modelled in part on the small-scale republican states which had been a feature of Northern India in the Buddha's time. For instance, explicit reference is made in the Pāli *Mahāparinibbāna Sutta* (DN 16) to the successful organisation of the republican Vajjis as a model to be emulated by the Buddhist Sangha. The Buddha himself was supposed to have come from a republican area. These areas were in the process of falling to the expanding kingdoms of the region, and ultimately, the Magadha kingdom where the Buddha had spent much of his teaching career, was built up into the Maurya Empire (321–184 BCE). Nonetheless, it seems that although the autonomous republics were integrated into kingdoms and empires, their structures were often left almost intact as units within the larger polity, so that they could be re-established where centralised control weakened, and some survived up until the fourth century CE. But the longest heritage of the organisational structure has been in the Buddhist Order.

In the Buddhist Sangha, ranking depends on the strict and automatic principle of age seniority, counted from the time of an individual's ordination. Community decision-making involves all senior monks, with great emphasis placed on the desirability of reaching unanimous decisions through consensus. In the absence of consensus, there are provisions for majority voting. Local Sanghas could form their own autonomous units. Moreover, even within a community, the rule emphasises a monk's own judgement, acknowledgement and admission of faults. Thus, any transgression should be publicly confessed by the monk himself prior to or during the communal gathering, and this in itself constitutes the purification of minor transgressions. More serious faults entail a period of suspension from the order. This approach was doctrinally related to the emphasis on intention: only an individual can judge whether they fully consciously and deliberately carried out the act and infringed the code. The persistence of the institution would suggest that its structure has great advantages, its involvement of the full community meaning that the institution remains responsive to its monk members, and the local autonomy also helpful in ensuring the continued active support of the local population. Moreover, it helps to avoid the possibility of radical transformations more likely in organisations subject to a centralised authority structure.

It is quite possible that the Buddha himself may have intended the conservatism built into the structure as a way of avoiding the take-over of the movement by a leader claiming charismatic authority. Certainly, the early Pāli texts give a picture of the Buddha declining to appoint a successor and pointing to his teachings and the monastic rule as validly representing him. The simple ranking system on the basis of seniority defined in terms of time since ordination limits the potential for an individual to claim authority over others on the basis of spiritual accomplishment. There are only four offences against the monastic code which result in permanent expulsion. It is significant in this respect that one of these most serious infringements is lying about spiritual attainments to lay people. It counts as a lesser offence to announce such attainments publicly if true. The raison d'être of the institution is to develop spiritual capabilities, and yet there was a strong impediment on the translation of such accomplishments into authority in the running of the monastic order. To some extent, this institutionalised approach may be modified in practice by the respect which spiritual teachers of great renown might inspire. In the Tibetan case, an able lama who chooses to leave a mark on his monastic organisation may do so. But quite often, a monastery's principal lamas will have little to do with its rather bureaucratic organisation, and lamas may even end up rather at the mercy of their monastic officials, who may seek to maximise the lamas' public teaching commitments in order to enhance the monastery's reputation and coffers.

In any case, building in non-hierarchical principles into the core of the organisational structure has helped to maintain the Buddhist order's viability and continuity in many contexts throughout its history. But the structure also has weaknesses. In particular, integration of the smaller units may be hard to maintain, and from the start, there was a tendency to divide. A group of four or more could form their own Sangha, while ten (or just five in border or foreign areas beyond the Indian heartlands) could become autonomous, able to perform their own ordination ceremonies. Each local Sangha was geographically defined, united by a commitment to gather regularly and recite the monastic rule. One unifying feature was that travelling monks would be expected to join the local gathering for this purpose. But any local variation in the ways of reciting the rules, which may have developed over time, or a dispute over any of the rules could lead to separately maintained lineages of ordination.

MONASTIC SCHOOLS

The early Buddhist 'schools', of which the Theravāda was just one, were associated with different ordination lines and geographical areas. They developed their own distinctive doctrinal positions although doctrinal splits did not necessarily lead to separate monasteries. The Mahāyāna, for instance, was not organisationally an independent order with its own ordination procedures. In India, Mahāyāna monks might reside in monasteries of different orders. In Northern and East Asian Buddhism, where Mahāyāna affiliation became the norm, the monastic ordination lineages generally remained those of the older schools. Thus, for instance, the Tibetans maintained the Mūlasarvāstivāda ordination procedures and the Chinese maintained the Dharmaguptaka vinaya. However, Japanese Buddhism provides an exception. Saichō (767–822), recognised as the founder of the Tendai school (based on Chinese Tiantai), produced an explicitly Mahāyāna ordination rite. Dōgen (1200–253) developed the code used by Zen monks, while other Japanese Buddhist teachers, such as Shinran

(1173–1263), founder of the True Pure Land School (see below), rejected monasticism altogether.

DECENTRALISED AND HIERARCHICAL STRUCTURES IN BUDDHIST MONASTICISM

A further implication of the decentralised structure of the Buddhist order was that difficulties might occur in dealing with groups of corrupt or ill-disciplined monks. The situation in which there is no centralised control, and in which individual monks are allowed to judge for themselves whether or not they have infringed the rules, lacks mechanisms for bringing degenerate factions into line. In most Buddhist countries, the egalitarian and non-hierarchical structure was to some extent subverted by the political control of monasteries, restricting the tendency for the Sangha to divide and, in some cases, actively purging groups of monks considered corrupt or divisive. The Emperor Aśoka himself (third century BCE) is supposed to have overseen a unification of the order, involving the expulsion of many monks. In fact, in Sri Lanka, it seems that support from secular authorities was often necessary to prevent lax discipline. When the nineteenth-century British Colonial Government withdrew from the traditional State role of protector of the Buddhist religion, the Sangha developed serious problems in its inability to control undisciplined monks. Nonetheless, in more recent times, the Sangha in Sri Lanka and Burma have valued the greater autonomy they have had due to their colonial disestablishment.

One recurring pattern which has occurred in Asian Buddhist countries is that there are allegations of corruption amongst monks, and where the State authorities are in a position to control the Sangha, they may impose periodic reforms or purifications. This demonstrates that upright behaviour continues to be seen as the ideal, but that the non-hierarchical structure may lack the ability to maintain monastic discipline.

Paradoxically, however, 'degeneration' from the monastic discipline in the sense of entanglements in worldly affairs becomes more likely when lay people make large offerings, monastic wealth accumulates, and complex administrative structures develop. Archaeological evidence seems to show that in ancient Indian Buddhism, not merely monastic institutions but even individual monks could end up with property and wealth in spite of the rule that monks should not possess gold or silver, a rule which became subject to rather different interpretations. There is some irony in this situation. The more 'pure' and upright a monastic group may be, the more it is likely to attract lay support, and hence gradually to become wealthy and powerful and then 'corrupt' from the viewpoint of the religious code. One striking example might be the dGe-lugs pa school in Tibet, who grew out of the bKa'-gdams pa movement which put particular stress on pure monastic discipline. The dGe-lugs pa initially became popular precisely because they had been untouched by the economic interests and power politics surrounding the more established monastic schools, but by the mid-seventeenth century, their prominence brought them into control over Government, as well as giving them vast monastic landholdings. From the mid-eighteenth to twentieth centuries their central monastic institutions became part of the State machinery.

This tendency towards monastic accumulation and increasing worldly involvements as a result of lay popularity occurs as a theme even in the lives and settlements of Buddhist meditator monks and hermits. Accounts of Sri Lankan and Thai forest meditator monks or Tibetan hermits frequently describe repeating scenarios of the reclusive meditator's willingness or need to come into contact with lay people for his food supplies and to give teaching, followed by steadily increasing numbers of devotees gathering around him, sometimes making rather excessive demands or simply embroiling him in activities, and then the opportunity to escape from the situation entirely and enter a new retreat. The theme may also be played out in accounts of important lamas who 'escape' from their monastic confines and find their real spiritual training and progress in meeting other spiritual masters, in pilgrimages and in secluded retreat. In the end, they may be re-integrated back into the monastic hierarchy as rather more effective and respected teachers than they started as, and it is almost as though the periods of breaking out seem an institutionalised and necessary component of the making of a great Buddhist teacher, who then may spend much of his career administering to the religious needs of students and of lay visitors.

In terms of the religious organisation, there are tensions between the two opposing tendencies of division and local autonomy, coupled with the absence of centralised control, versus greater discipline and integration, linked, however, to political and/or economic interests either in terms of subjection to rulers or of becoming an independent player in the world of the political economy. Throughout Asian Buddhism we find many examples of each of these poles, sometimes in the same cultural environment. In Tibet, for instance, small-scale slightly disorganised groupings could be found alongside large-scale monastic hierarchies.

MONASTERIES AND THE POLITICAL ECONOMY

It would seem that monastic property and involvement in economic activities was commonplace in early Indian Buddhism. There is archaeological evidence for monks participating in trade and, apparently, even the minting of coins in monasteries (Schopen 1997: 5, 18 note 27). Internationally, too, with the spread of Buddhism, monasteries found a niche within the social, economic and political structures, such that until modern times, especially in Northern and Southern Buddhist countries, Buddhist monasteries had large landholdings and an important role in local and national political organisation.

In part, the situation developed through the patronage and protection of kings and rulers sympathetic to Buddhism. The early texts had shown the Buddha as an adviser and teacher of kings and princes, and the rulers were portrayed as generous benefactors and, in some cases, serious spiritual practitioners. The Buddha had encouraged an ethos which moved from Brahmanical ideas concerning the ruler's duty, such as the performance of sacrifices, to a focus on the overall social good. The example of the Emperor Aśoka was important in the development of the model of the ideal monarch who supports and promotes the Sangha and Buddhist values while, in turn, monasteries would help to legitimise the just rule of the king. In time, different Asian countries developed their own models on the basis of kings who had played a part in establishing Buddhism in their regions.

BUDDHISM AND JUST RULE

Peter Skilling notes that there have been a variety of models for government in line with Buddhism. The first names he lists are rulers who the Buddha was said to have advised:

> ... poor Asoka is trotted out mechanically whenever kingship is discussed. There is no denying his pervasive influence over the centuries, but is it not time to consider the role of other rulers, such as Bimbisara, Prasenajit, or Ajatasatru? We must also not forget that historical rulers become quasi-legendary paradigms – the Chos rgyals in Tibet, for example, or Anawratha and Bayinnaung in Burma, or "Phra Ruang" in Siam – and exert their own influences on their successors.
>
> (Peter Skilling 1997 *Journal of the American Oriental Society*, 117 no. 3: 579–80)

There is another aspect of the expansion of monastic wealth which is equally important. It is perhaps not coincidental that the periods when the build-up of Buddhist monasticism gained momentum both in the Tibetan-speaking regions and in China were times of weakened centralised political control. In the Chinese case, it was the *period of disunity* (311–589); in the Tibetan case, the Post-Imperial period after the collapse of the State in the mid-ninth century began the process, which went much further from the eleventh century when regional kings and rulers started to sponsor Buddhist monasteries during what is called the *New Translation period*.

What is most striking about these periods in China and Tibet is either the absence of centralised political power or its limited authority. The situation is perhaps not unlike the expansion of Christian monasteries in Medieval Europe, when local barons might have had real power and the centralised State was comparatively weak. In these circumstances, religious authorities might rise to prominence as advisers, mediators and arbitrators. Certainly, mediation of disputes was one of the principal tasks for lamas throughout Tibetan history. It was in their capacity as mediators helping to negotiate peace, first between neighbouring aristocratic rulers and then in the mid-thirteenth century between Mongols and Tibetans, that the political influence of lamas and the wealth of monasteries grew throughout the Tibetan region. The comparative strength of the monasteries in Northern Buddhism, and especially in Tibet, Ladakh and in the eastern areas of the Tibetan plateau, which were for much of the time beyond the effective control either of the Chinese or the Tibetan State, is also related to the relative weakness of State control. In Southern Buddhist contexts, the kings tended to patronise yet keep the religious authorities under control. In China, the State had an uneasy relationship with Buddhist monasteries and often sought to limit their influence. In Tibet, by contrast, monastic power increased over the centuries at the expense of the aristocracy, and it effectively limited State control, even during the nineteenth to twentieth centuries when the State was modernising and extending the domains of its authority.

GENDER STRATIFICATION IN ASIAN BUDDHIST PRACTICE

There now tends to be agreement in Religious Studies that gender issues should be addressed, but less agreement on the facts of the relationship between the religion and the social position of men and women in the religion, and even less agreement on the causes for gender inequalities in religion, in culture more generally or in society.

We need to seek a nuanced understanding not only of the religious doctrines and what impact they may or may not have on the religious practice, but also of the relationship of the religion to other cultural traditions and to the social and economic structures of the society.

PROBLEMS OF INTERPRETATION

There are no obvious single causes for more or less gender inequality. We find great variations within societies, cultural groups, religious traditions. Above all, it is not necessarily clear in which circumstances women will be more – or less – restricted. One need only consider debates over the Veil in Islam, or female monasticism in Buddhism, Jainism, or Christianity. Monasticism may be seen as restricting women's full participation in social or religious decision-making. Others argue that it can take attention off women as sexual objects, free them from family and social constraints, allowing them autonomy to develop spiritually.

Analysing such situations may be very difficult. There are particular difficulties when we examine doctrine or theology and its relation to religious practice. Feminists sometimes assume that female imagery may reflect women's involvement in its creation and will at the very least help to promote women's participation in the spiritual path. Yet sometimes feminine imagery may be linked to particularly male-dominated religious systems and the imagery may do less to reflect women's religious aspirations than men's stereotyped images of idealised femininity. Conversely, male imagery may be susceptible to female use. In Mahāyāna Buddhism, the imagery of the female bodhisattva Tārā may be linked to women's spiritual aspirations – for example, there is the story that she vowed to become enlightened as a woman. But also Tārā's popularity amongst male monastics may be related to her portrayal as a protective mother and as a morally pure, beautiful and perfect woman bestowing unconditional love, a male ideal rather than a real woman. So we need some caution in interpreting the picture of male and female figures found in religious teachings.

A further complexity may relate to gaps between ideology and practice. The epigraphical evidence for the beginnings and development of the use of Buddha images seems to demonstrate there was significant involvement of nuns in the early centuries CE (Gregory Schopen 1997: 238–57). Moreover, these nuns were often apparently highly erudite scholars, not lowly followers, and they took significant roles in sponsoring and organising the establishment of large images in important Buddhist sites. Female involvement, however, seems rather dramatically to have faded away during the Gupta period (320–500), at the same time that the Mahāyāna was becoming a popular movement. So, on the face of it, Mahāyāna doctrine, as we saw above, which would appear more favourable to female spiritual practice, is becoming established just at a time when female participation has become less fully equal than it had been. How might we explain such a discrepancy? Perhaps it is most likely that women's involvement was restricted by the greater socioeconomic structural constraints which were in evidence in Gupta times. During the Gupta era, caste regulations in Indian society became more rigid and were backed up by political and legal sanctions. Notions of the irrelevance of gender in the spiritual path, as expressed in Mahāyāna sūtras, might have been developed as a challenge to monk practitioners' fixed views or to the prevalent social attitudes, without having any real impact on the social norms. Indeed, a teaching of gender equality would have been much harder hitting in a context where women's choices were in practice very limited. Gender ideologies, then, need not necessarily have any great impact on social realities.

FORMAL STRUCTURES VERSUS INFORMAL INFLUENCE

In analysing such complex relations between doctrine and practice, the scholar needs to distinguish between formal structures of authority and the informal exercise of power or influence. It can be the case that in practice, women may be able to gain influence and even take control of religious decision-making where on the face of it they utterly lack the resources or the formal status to do so. They may be able to influence or even manipulate the men occupying the ostensible formal positions of authority. The assumptions of the early feminist era that formal male dominance must be 'good' for men and 'bad' for women is often debatable. Formal positions of authority in some cases may be stressful and create a good deal of responsibility without actually bringing many tangible rewards in terms of social recognition. For example, a male priest may have a higher theoretical status than a female diviner, but the diviner may have more real social power and influence and even, in some cases, greater financial reward for her services. There is therefore a tendency in contemporary studies of women in religion to focus less on the formal structures of the religious system and more on what women actually make of the roles they take within it.

RELIGION AND SOCIAL INVOLVEMENTS

In looking at these issues in relation to Buddhism, it is worth first re-visiting the discussion in Chapter 2 of variation in the extent to which a religion seeks to apply its ethical principles in the wider social sphere beyond its specifically religious organisation. As we have seen, there is a large difference, at least in theory, between Islam and Buddhism in this respect. This can work both ways in terms of the impact of the religion on society. For instance, in some past historical situations, the insistence in Islam on some specified if limited provision for female inheritance and a clear statement of husbands' duties towards wives might have had some effect in modifying harsh aspects of pre-modern Arab social structures from women's perspective. Buddhism's official lack of comment about gender relations in the wider society may appear a comparative failure in comparable circumstances although, admittedly, oppressive social and family relations would hardly fit comfortably with Buddhist moral standards. But matters look different where the society is more egalitarian. Perhaps in the contemporary situation where gender roles in many societies are changing rapidly and becoming more equal, a religion's silence or ready acceptance may be seen as more progressive than upholding a proscriptive template sanctioned by scripture.

THE NUNS' ORDER AND BUDDHIST APPROACHES TO THE SPIRITUAL PATH

When shifting our attention to the specifically religious organisation, it is worth saying that – as we witness in the case of the decline of women's participation in Buddhism during the Gupta period – we might expect a religion generally to reflect the wider social and cultural environment it finds itself in. Nonetheless, the religion may represent a particularly conservative streak in society, maintaining gender inequalities in religious organisation even when they have been abandoned elsewhere. By the same token, a religion may innovate in a progressive fashion. The establishment of Jain and Buddhist orders for nuns at around the same time, very early in the development of the two traditions, would seem to suggest this. That women achieved a formally recognised structure for spiritual training is explicitly related to Buddhism's teaching on the equality of men and women in relation to their spiritual potential to achieve Enlightenment. This ethical and spiritual universalism was of course an important component of Buddhist doctrine, and it has remained significant in the recognition of women's spiritual achievements at various times. The Theravāda have preserved an account of early female practitioners of renown. The archaeological record would seem to indicate that women in the early centuries CE could have their exceptional Buddhist scholarship and influence recognised, and although stories of female Buddhist masters and saints are not as common as those about men, they do occur.

WOMEN'S SPIRITUAL POTENTIAL

The story of the founding of the nuns' order makes it clear that the Buddha affirmed the potential of women to attain Enlightenment:

So he [Ānanda] said to the Blessed One, "Venerable sir, if a woman were to go forth from the home life into homelessness in the doctrine and discipline made known by the Tathāgata, would she be able to realize the fruit of stream-entry, once-returning, non-returning, or arahantship?" "Yes, Ānanda, she would ... " The Pāli Vinaya, Cullavagga 10.

(www.accesstoinsight.org/lib/authors/thanissaro/bmc2/bmc2.ch23.html)

At the same time, there is also a strand found in various sources which would seem to play down or undermine universalism, suggesting that women have special difficulties in dealing with their emotions or in training the mind. Such sentiments may even be expressed in accounts of female saints said to have attained Enlightenment. Having said that, it seems that such comments are not always to be taken at face value. The autobiographical reflections of the early twentieth-century female Tibetan tantric master, Se-ra mKha'-'gro, studied by Sarah Jacoby, express reservations about her abilities due to her gender. Yet these disguise a quiet assertiveness, providing the means for her to show the expected Buddhist virtue of humility, at the same time as invoking the contrary reaffirmations from her male lamas and spiritual friends.

Nonetheless, the assumption that women are in some sense inherently less capable of spiritual progress than men can persist despite the exceptional cases. Moreover, women are frequently presented in texts intended for monks as liable to engender lust and distract them from their spiritual path. Similar points may be made about attachment to men from the female perspective, but since far more texts relate the problems of male rather than female monastics, a balanced overall impression is not created. Furthermore, there may be a subtle difference in the presentation of the accounts of female practitioners in contrast to some of the stories for monks. The nuns in the stories of the early Theravāda Elder Nuns generally seem only to reflect on the unsatisfactory and impermanent nature of their *own* beauty and bodies or of the beauty of other women (Pruitt 1998: 101–13, 260–62). Teachings aimed at monks may similarly encourage contemplation of the impermanence of the meditator's own body, but the nuns do not also dwell on the illusory attractiveness of the man's body in the way which may be found in teachings on the allure of the female body for men.

A wide range of sources, including Mahāyāna sūtras, express the notion that a woman's birth is inferior, the result of less good karma than a male human birth, and women would do better to be reborn as men. In societies where women have limited choices and less chance to lead a religious career, a negative judgement on women's fate might be thought simply to reflect empirical reality. Yet the distinction between recognition of actual gender inequalities and comment on women's innate nature is not always made clear.

THE NUNS' ORDER IN HISTORY

The female equivalent of the full monk's status was supposedly established through the appeal of the Buddha's aunt/step-mother, who soon afterwards attained Enlightenment, and her five hundred companions who ordained beside her were also reputed to have achieved high spiritual attainments (Pruitt 1998: 182). The vinaya account of the official beginnings of the nun's order, as it is preserved in the Pāli tradition (Vinaya, Cullavaga 10), is nonetheless hedged in with caveats about the need for nuns to accept extra rules and the detrimental effect of the entry of nuns on the lifespan of the order as a whole. Modern textual criticism (see Liz Williams 2000 and 2002) would suggest that the final sections relating to the added rules and the effects of the nuns' admission are likely to have been later additions to the text. Moreover, the formulation, together with other stories elsewhere, such as references to the existence of the nuns' order while the Buddha's aunt was still a laywoman, would seem to presuppose the prior existence of nuns, suggesting that the account relates more to the codification of the rules for nuns. As in the case of the monks' ordination and rule, the first 'ordinations' were simple and informal, but later, more detailed and elaborate procedures were instigated. The final comment about the detrimental impact of the nuns' community is contradicted by many other scriptural references which emphasise the responsibility placed on all monastics, since their failure to uphold the teaching will bring about its degeneration and decline. Moreover, other passages suggest that the nuns – and lay people also – were from the outset envisaged as an integral part of the community as a whole.

For instance, the *Mahāparinibānna Sutta* (DN 16) has it that Māra reminds the Buddha that he had refused to pass away following his Enlightenment until he had established the four groups (monks, nuns, laymen and women) on the path, and that has now been achieved.

Thus, the cautionary tone of this charter myth for the nuns' order does not fit altogether comfortably with the ethos of a good deal of the early texts on nuns, their attainments and the encouragement given to them by the Buddha. To make sense of the apparent discrepancy in these approaches, we should not rely simply on the idea that we have an earlier more positive strand with a later editorial layer imposed on it. After all, the passages from elsewhere in the collected scriptures were themselves surely subjected to editorial interventions, yet they lack similar qualification. We must return to the point made in the discussion of monastic organisation above that we witness a clear distinction between spiritual progress and attainment on one hand and the structural order of the Sangha, which institutionalised an automatic ranking system based on egalitarian – or republican – and bureaucratic principles. Assuming that the charter myth is indeed primarily concerned with codification of the nuns' rule, the text's focus on the eight special rules is important not as a comment on nuns' spiritual capacities but rather on their structural relation to the order of monks. The clear message here is that the nuns are to be structurally subordinate to the monks, no matter what their spiritual attainment or standing in the community. In short, a straightforward gender stratification is built into the formal structure of the Buddhist Sangha, irrespective of the individual qualities of monks and nuns.

It is hard to say how far – if at all – this formal organisation in itself impacted detrimentally on the long-term viability of the nuns' order. Historically, however, the nuns' order proved more vulnerable than that of the monks to the vagaries of the social and economic support systems on which the Buddhist order depended. 'Nuns' in the sense of full-time female monastics survived right across Buddhist Asia, but the lineage of the full nuns' ordination only survived in East Asian Buddhism. Even here, it was fairly weak until modern times, and it is quite possible that there had been interruptions to its continuity and the need for its revival. In Southern Buddhism, the fully ordained nuns' order seems to have died out in the eleventh century CE; it perhaps held on until the thirteenth century in Burma. The lineage was never established in Tibet, so it has been altogether absent in Northern Buddhism, despite the existence of translations into Tibetan of the textual sources on the nuns' code.

THE NUNS' ORDER AND FEMALE SPIRITUAL PRACTICE TODAY

In the last few decades, there has been a movement to re-establish the nuns' ordination lineage in all the traditions, on the basis of the extant lineages preserved in Taiwan and Korea. This has created new contacts and interchange between nuns from different traditions, but it has also caused controversy and opposition in Southern and Northern Buddhist contexts. There is the problem of nuns from their traditions having recourse to a monastic lineage descending from a different school and also the traditionally problematic possibility that that lineage might have been broken. The matter has been especially divisive in Southern Buddhist countries where there is an added concern over what is seen as relative laxity in monastic discipline in Mahāyāna countries. But the issue is not only one of modernists versus traditional authorities. Many Asian Buddhist nuns are opposed to the introduction of the lineage, and it seems that the distinction between formal and informal status is relevant here. The opponents have little interest in introducing a new formal status, which in any case may be dubious from the perspective of their particular tradition and which may appear as a challenge to their monastic authorities, unseemly in terms of Buddhist virtues. They may prefer to work with their monk mentors and colleagues informally to improve the actual status and role which they already have, in a way which is beneficial for their Sangha and community as a whole (see Hiroko Kawanami 2007). In Northern Buddhism, there has been less controversy, and the ordination movement has secured the Dalai Lama's enthusiastic support, although it has so far been a minority interest.

Regardless of their secondary status, and in many Buddhist countries not even having the formal position of fully ordained nuns, full-time women practitioners have played a significant part in religious life throughout Buddhist Asia. In Burma, for instance, there are about thirty thousand nuns. Nuns have supportive roles in the monastic community, such as handling the donation money which monks are not allowed to touch, helping with preparations for rituals, and taking responsibility for the welfare of monks and novices. They also study and teach. In the twentieth century, increasing numbers of nuns have gained formal teaching qualifications and many new nunnery schools have opened. So nuns may have much informal influence, even if they are considered as inferior to monks.

In South Korea, the number of fully ordained Buddhist nuns is similar to that of monks, and nuns have been actively involved in Buddhist revival. Buddhism in Korea had been restricted during the Neo-Confucian Choson dynasty (late fourteenth to early twentieth century), and this was followed by the period of Japanese occupation which had had a further detrimental impact on Korean Buddhism and especially on its celibate monasticism, which was discouraged. From the mid-twentieth century, Buddhist monasticism has had a resurgence. Nuns receive a thorough college training and also have the possibility of intensive meditation training and practice. They have their own institutions, and they also take part in joint ceremonies and communal events with monks.

A similar revival of monasticism has taken place in Taiwan in the Post-War period, with full ordination and opportunities to study, practise and teach Buddhism being open to women. Nuns today outnumber monks but this is not considered a happy situation by nuns, since it indicates the weakness of male monasticism, in a context where parents would not generally support sons becoming monks and there are good secular choices for men. But it has meant that nuns have had the chance to fulfil important organisational roles as well as having autonomy and choice in their religious practice.

Tibetan nuns had a status equivalent to that of novices and, in formal terms, were traditionally quite restricted in their options. There were few nunneries in comparison with the numbers of monasteries and most institutions for nuns were less well-funded junior partners of monasteries. There was virtually no possibility for nuns to train in the monastic colleges. But there were large numbers of nuns, most of whom remained at home. Some became itinerant or entered reclusive meditation retreats. Despite institutionalised inequality, nuns might have the chance to take an active part in local religious activities. Nuns, and indeed lay women, could receive tantric teachings and, in exceptional cases, could even become tantric masters and teachers in their own right. Now in exile in India, many small nunneries have been established and young nuns are often able to secure international sponsors. With the Dalai Lama's encouragement, training in philosophy has been opened to nuns and nuns have greater opportunities to study than they once did. In Tibet, nuns have played an important part in religious reconstruction since the 1980s.

BEYOND THE MONASTERY

Following early role models of the Buddha's first lay disciples and sponsors, women have been active as lay patrons in all Buddhist societies and, as such, may also have had some impact on the religious community. The extent to which non-monastics could receive religious training and participate in spiritual practices was, of course, variable in the different regions. In Tibetan Buddhism, women were important as mothers and wives in the hereditary lama lineages, and sometimes daughters of the family would also take on religious roles. They would not often have the formal lama's title, but the women of the family would generally be trained in the religious practices in which their involvement might effectively be required. The spiritual dependency of a tantric lama on his consort or wife is quite explicit in the textual sources. The lesser status mantra practitioner communities similarly trained women as well as men.

In short, structural gender inequalities often place restraints on Asian Buddhist women's full formal participation in religious life, but in practice, women's active involvements may modify the impact of such inequalities. In Tibet, there have been many cases of individual women coming to prominence through their religious activities. For example, the early twentieth-century Se-ra mKha'-'gro became famous for her meditational achievements. She was recognised as a lineage bearer of important tantric transmissions and also revealed her own cycle of tantric scriptures. Perhaps, just as impressively, she was rather prolific as a scholar, editing the collected works of her lama husband and his father, and composing commentaries on them, even though she had not received a formal education. In the late twentieth century, a charismatic female meditation adept in 'Bri-gung, Tibet, established herself in an apparently traditional position for a recognised emanation of the eighth-century female

Buddhist saint Ye-shes mtsho-rgyal, and recreated a nuns' community and revitalised religious practice in the area. Similarly, in the Thai forest tradition, a woman meditator, teacher and poet, who appears to have been known by a title which simply means a female lay follower (Upasika Kee Nanayon 1901–79), founded a centre for women meditators in 1945 and came to have a great reputation, such that she is known beyond Thailand and a number of publications of her teachings have been translated and published in English.

CHAPTER SUMMARY

- The Buddhist monastic code expresses an ideal of mutual dependency between monastics and lay people; the Middle Way principle is expressed in the rules and the idea of the Rule as the spiritual path is echoed in other Buddhist sets of precepts, for bodhisattvas and for mantra practitioners.
- The Sangha has the task of maintaining meditative accomplishments, the scriptural and scholarly transmission, and of teaching and performing religious services.
- Buddhism has some non-monastic religious specialists, of importance in East Asian and Tibetan Buddhism.
- In early Mahāyāna, there was some explicit challenge of the opposition between monk and lay, but this did not translate into less stratified social practice.
- There may be much community involvement in the local monastery; the monastic organisation reflects the ancient Indian Republics, resulting in separate monastic orders, but the classic organisation may be modified by the wider political structure.
- Historically, Buddhist monasteries played a crucial part in Asian political economies.
- Issues of gender stratification have complexities such as gaps between doctrine and practice, formal and informal authority, and relations between the religion and wider society and culture.
- In Buddhism, there was a doctrine of spiritual gender equality but structural inequality in organisation.
- The nuns' order was historically weak; there are moves to revive it in all traditions now but some nuns prefer to focus on improving the status of nuns without formal ordination; some women have gained respect for meditation accomplishments.

FURTHER READING

Bechert, Heinz and Richard Gombrich (eds) 1984 *The World of Buddhism: Buddhist Monks and Nuns in Society and Culture*. This collection contains useful discussions of Buddhist monasticism and society in Asia.

Chikwang Sunim 1999 'A Strong Tradition Adapting to Change: The Nuns in Korea'. A short article on Korean nuns by a Korean-trained Australian nun.

Goldstein, Melvyn C. and Matthew Kapstein 1998 *Buddhism in Contemporary Tibet: Religious Revival and Cultural Identity*. The articles by David Germano and Matthew Kapstein discuss the female adept in 'Bri gung.

Gombrich, Richard 2006 *Theravāda Buddhism*. Helpful on the Sangha in ancient India as well as developments in Sri Lanka.

Gyatso, Janet 'A Partial Genealogy of the Lifestory of Ye shes mtsho rgyal.' A discussion about the stories of a Tibetan culture heroine.

Jacoby, Sarah '"This Inferior Female Body:" Reflections on Life as a Treasure Revealer Through the Autobiographical Eyes of Se ra mKha' 'gro (bde ba'i rdo rje, 1892–1940).' A fascinating account of a Tibetan woman who became a renowned lama.

Kawanami, Hiroko 2007 'The Bhikkhunī Ordination Debate: Global Aspirations, Local Concerns, with Special Emphasis on the Views of the Monastic Community in Burma'. A sensitive treatment of controversies surrounding the reintroduction of the nuns' ordination lineage in Burma.

Kee Nanayon, Upasika 2003 'Pure and Simple'. Short extract of teaching by a Thai female meditation adept.

Pruitt, William 1998 *Commentary on Verses of Therīs*. Stories of early Buddhist spiritually advanced and Enlightened nuns, preserved in Pāli.

Samuel, Geoffrey 1993 *Civilized Shamans: Buddhism in Tibetan Societies*. Gives a good account of historical relations between political power and monasteries in Tibetan and Himalayan areas.

Schopen, Gregory 1997 *Bones, Stones, and Buddhist Monks*. An interesting collection of articles examining the archaeological evidence concerning early Buddhist practice and monasticism.

Tsomo, Karma Lekshe (ed.) *Sakyadhīta: Daughters of the Buddha*. Articles on nuns in different Asian countries.

Williams, Liz 2000 'A Whisper in the Silence: Nuns before Mahāpajāpatī?' and 2002 'Red Rust, Robbers and Rice Fields: Women's Part in the Precipitation of the Decline of the Dhamma'. Two articles on the early Buddhist nuns' order, critically examining the Theravāda textual account.

5

THE MAJOR BUDDHIST TRADITIONS

CLASSIFICATIONS AND DEFINITIONS: THEIR USES AND LIMITATIONS

The main extant Buddhist groupings have been referred to throughout the book under the umbrella regional categories of Southern, Northern and East Asian Buddhism, and with reference to the Theravāda and Mahāyāna traditions of religious transmission. These categories are helpful to gain an understanding of the important contrasts between different kinds of Buddhist doctrine and practice but they simplify a complex picture of affiliation, overlap and variation.

Once it was common in Religious Studies to look for the essence of a religion and to seek to characterise it accordingly. Thus, the question might be asked, 'What are the essential characteristics of Buddhism?' More recently, rejection of essentialism and focus instead on diversity has swung the pendulum to the opposite pole, and the idea of 'multiple Buddhisms' is heard in university classrooms. Perhaps a 'middle way' makes most sense. As we have seen in this book, there are features of Buddhist ethical principles, doctrine, meditative and ritual practice which are widely shared or could be seen as variants on the same theme in at least the mainstream Buddhist traditions. However, how these are applied in practice may vary considerably and even in one country and tradition, there may be opposing interpretations of Buddhist teachings. It is also hard to pin down key specific features that are universal to Buddhism and which could work as defining characteristics either of Buddhism or even of any of its major traditions. The traditional decentralised nature of the Buddhist order and the lack of integrating hierarchical authorities to speak for Buddhists or for major denominations of Buddhism does not help in this respect. These points would be true even before the twenty-first century. In today's world, with adaptations of established traditions to new geographical areas and new social structural settings, such as modern cities, along with the rise of new Buddhist movements, defining features may seem more elusive. At the same time, increased international communication between different Buddhist traditions has brought interest in religious exchange and in finding areas of common ground. Such exchanges are not always limited simply to increasing knowledge of each other's tradition but may entail real involvements, such as nuns from one tradition receiving full ordination in another where it is available.

HISTORICAL OVERVIEW OF THE MAJOR REGIONS OF BUDDHISM IN ASIA

LIMITATIONS TO THE THREE-REGION MODEL

THE CENTRAL ASIAN CASE

The threefold division we have been using has some merit in epitomising the principal Buddhist traditions over the past thousand years. However, it is worth remembering that Buddhism in Asia stretches back historically much further than this. For well over a thousand years, it developed in the Indian subcontinent. Most of the common scriptural heritage and many of the shared traditions of practice – monasticism, aspects of temple design, pilgrimage, rites of veneration, meditation, to name a few – derive from the first centuries of Buddhism in India.

India is unlikely to be forgotten, either in Buddhist countries or in studies of Buddhism, but there is one region that was once in the forefront of Buddhist development, but which is not represented in the three major regions, and that is Central Asia. Had Central Asia not been so entirely overwhelmed by the advance of Islam might we have had a further major Asian Buddhist region? Or might it have progressed along similar lines to Northern Buddhism? It is impossible to say. As it is, we can note that Central Asian contributions had an important impact especially on East Asian and Northern Buddhism in their formative stages. In the third century BCE, the Indian Maurya Empire helped to spread Buddhism northwards. The use of images in Buddhist worship began in the north. Gandhāra, situated in modern-day northern Pakistan and eastern Afghanistan, was one of the birth places of this development around the turn of the Christian era. The extent of Buddhist practice in its heyday in this region may be judged by the cave monasteries such as the third- to fifth-century site at Bāmiyān in present-day Afghanistan, where massive stone Buddha images were carved out of the sides of the cliffs. During the Kuṣāṇa Empire (60–240 CE), Buddhism was enthusiastically patronised by the kings, who ruled a large area stretching across much of Central Asia, northern India, and parts of Chinese Turkestan. In this time of stability, Buddhism travelled east along the Silk routes to China, and cultural interchange continued for many centuries. Most of the early translations of Buddhist texts into Chinese are associated with Central Asian monk scholars. Many of the smaller-scale kingdoms that followed after the Kuṣāṇa period continued to allow Buddhism to prosper. The kingdoms or city states of Kāshgar, Kucha and Khotan, important for the Silk route trade, were centres of Buddhist culture for several centuries. In the seventh century, the Tibetans expanded into Central Asia, briefly taking control of the trade routes. Initially, this represented damage to the Buddhism of these areas but, in the longer term, the Central Asians had a significant cultural impact on the Tibetans, as the Tibetan Empire began to patronise Buddhism and other literary cultural traditions of their neighbours. Central Asia had a range of Buddhist groupings, but the Dharmaguptaka monastic order was important, with the Sarvāstivāda monastic order later becoming dominant. The region was also central in the rise of Mahāyāna and in the development of bodhisattva imagery. The cult of the Buddha Amitābha rose to prominence in this area. But by the second millennium CE, Buddhism in Central Asia had lost its position and never recovered it.

OTHER COMPLEXITIES AND ANOMALIES

The Indonesian islands represent another area where Buddhism was historically important. Along with Hinduism, various Buddhist traditions were gradually introduced from the early centuries CE and patronised by many of the kings. Tantric influence is seen in the huge *stūpa* and *maṇḍala* (sacred circle) complex at Borobudur in Java. Buddhism here later became syncretised with Hinduism. The situation was similar in parts of mainland South-east Asia at this time, and had Buddhism survived in Indonesia, it is even just possible that it would have taken part in the trajectory which led to the dominance of Theravāda Buddhism on the mainland. However, Islam was introduced from the thirteenth century and became the dominant religion by the seventeenth century.

A further problem with summing up the diversity of Buddhism under the threefold division is that in the early periods of Buddhism's expansion into the three areas, they witnessed the presence of traditions other than those which became dominant over time. Thus, historically each region may have been less uniform than it later appeared. Each area can also be divided into its own regions, with local socio-cultural traditions and political or economic circumstances impacting on the practice of Buddhism.

Moreover, the large geographical areas have some overlaps and pockets of other affiliation. Thus, Vietnam, which geographically would fit within South-east Asia, has historically had close contact with China, and East Asian traditions have been more prevalent there, especially in the north (see below).

There are also a few anomalies which do not fit neatly into any of the three groupings. For example, the Newars of Nepal have historically maintained close links with Tibetans and they also have tantric traditions of practice, but their practice is based on Sanskrit tantric texts, rather than Tibetan translations, and a separate transmission from late Indian Buddhism. Given historical political pressures, they also abandoned celibate monasticism and adapted their religious organisation accordingly. Finally, there are perhaps several million *Ambedkar Buddhists* in India, concentrated in Maharashtra, mostly formerly low caste Hindus who have converted – often en masse – to Buddhism from the mid-twentieth century. Ambedkar promoted a modernist form of Buddhism focused on social action rather than the meditative teachings or traditional practices of 'merit making'.

SOUTHERN BUDDHISM: SRI LANKA, BURMA, THAILAND, CAMBODIA AND LAOS

Many academic books on Buddhism start with Southern Buddhism in considering the three regions. One reason for this convention is that, historically, the first major international expansion to one of our three areas for which we have good evidence was the mission during the reign of the Mauryan Emperor Aśoka to Sri Lanka in the third century BCE. Moreover, the early Pāli *sutta* and *vinaya* scriptures give us the most complete view of early Buddhism found in textual sources. Parallel texts from other early traditions are preserved in Chinese, but the Chinese translations of these do not continue to play such a central role in East Asian Buddhism as the early Pāli texts play in the Theravāda tradition of Sri Lanka and South-east Asia. The authority of the earliest texts remains undiminished in Southern Buddhism, and Theravāda teachers pride themselves on their closeness to the earliest Buddhist heritage.

Nonetheless, the convention should not be mistaken for a judgement that Southern Buddhism as a whole represents an early unchanged tradition from which the other regions departed. The Theravāda order derives from one branch of the early Buddhist tradition, that of the *Elders*, *Sthavira* in Sanskrit (= Pāli *Thera*). In the first formal division of the Buddhist monastic order, perhaps a century after the Buddha's passing, the Sthaviras split from the *Great Assembly* (*Mahāsaṃghika*, see Chapter 2), the Elders favouring a stricter interpretation of the monastic rule. The Elders themselves divided into different groups, including the Sarvāstivāda (see above), who were most well established in the North of India and later in Central Asia, and the Theravāda, who became rooted in Sri Lanka. It is hard to say which of the early groups was closest to the original teaching and practice. Over the centuries, some contacts between the different orders continued, but the Theravāda developed a good deal of their commentarial tradition in Sri Lanka, and they did not take part in the later developments of Buddhism in the areas to the north and elsewhere in the Indian subcontinent.

The Theravāda Pāli texts were first committed to writing in the first century BCE in Sri Lanka. The precise content of the Pāli

Canon was established in Sri Lanka by the fifth century CE. There is some uncertainty over the timing of the late additions, but the earlier texts had been fixed long before and the general contours of the collection had been shaped by the end of the third century CE. The fourth- or fifth-century Buddhaghoṣa, drawing on commentaries which had earlier been composed in Sinhalese, perhaps drawing on Indian originals, wrote what became the most influential commentaries in Pāli. Over several centuries following, Sinhalese commentators added to the heritage.

In Southern Buddhism, the Pāli vinaya is maintained along with its principles of the interdependency between monks and lay people, as discussed in Chapter 4. These were, however, modified by the political control over the monastic order when and where governments were in the position to do so, and also by the economic power of monastic institutions, which often became land owners and socio-political authorities in their own right, as also referred to in Chapter 4. In these South and South-east Asian societies, local religious and cultural traditions often also kept an important place in everyday life. The religious specialists of the folk traditions generally had lower status than the monks, but might have considerable influence in the community, dealing with affairs which the monks had no part in.

SRI LANKA

Only one line of the three early Buddhist establishments of ancient Anurādhapura in Sri Lanka survived, the Mahāvihāra. In the twelfth century, the three were unified by the king under the Mahāvihāra. Before that, the other two had had long rivalries with the Mahāvihāra. The Abhayagiri seem to have been more open to influences from India, such as the Mahāyāna. In any case, the Sri Lankan base did not mean that Buddhism on the island became completely insular. Buddhism persisted for longer in South India than in the north, there were monk visitors from India, and contacts maintained with other Asian countries. For instance, the monastic lineage was established in Burma and then re-introduced back to Sri Lanka from there after a troubled period in the early eleventh century, when the nun's ordination lineage was lost.

In later centuries, Buddhism continued to be central to Sinhalese cultural and national identity although, at times, political problems made the monastic lineage fragile, and more than once again, it was brought back from Southest Asia. The island was not always politically unified. There had been periodic South Indian Tamil incursions since early times, a Tamil kingdom centred on Jaffna in the north between the thirteenth and seventeenth century, and the north became a predominantly Tamil ethnic area, mostly but not exclusively practising Hindu traditions. After the development of European political and economic interests in Sri Lanka from the sixteenth century, the Theravāda monastic lineage was re-introduced from Thailand in the eighteenth century, and the contemporary order largely derives from this transmission. British Colonial rule from the early nine-teenth century had an impact on Buddhism, in the disestablishment of the Sangha, other aspects of modernisation, the involvement of Buddhism with nationalist aspirations, as well as the need to respond to Christian missionaries.

SOUTH-EAST ASIA

Like Java, the South–east Asian countries which became Theravāda introduced various Hindu traditions alongside different forms of Buddhism. However, unlike Java, Buddhism did not merge into Hindu practice, and a Buddhist identity became important to the region's peoples.

South–east Asian Buddhism has some features which set it apart from Sri Lankan Theravāda practice. For instance, a tradition of temporary ordination almost as a rites-de-passage for young men means that perhaps half of the male population in Burma and Thailand has been in the order. Also, some themes in Buddhist narratives and artistic imagery which are preserved in South–east Asia are not now in evidence in Sri Lanka although they may be found in Sanskrit traditions.

The modern nation states of Burma, Thailand, Cambodia and Laos do not correspond neatly to political or ethnic units of the past. There were complex interconnections between many small political entities, alongside political centres with fluctuating levels of control over surrounding areas which were often peopled by diverse ethnicities. This should be remembered in reading the country overviews here. Southern Buddhism has also been present in neighbouring areas of other modern states:

- Amongst the Dai minority nationality of Xishuangbanna (also called Sipsongpanna) in China's south-western Yunnan Province, where Theravāda was established in the fifteenth century.
- In the Chittagong district of Bangladesh, although, in this case, traditional forms of Buddhism had been local variants of tantric Northern Buddhist practices, while Theravāda Buddhism was introduced in a nineteenth-century reforming movement.
- In Indian border regions, there are groups of Southern Buddhists, such as small communities of Tai Theravāda Buddhists in the north-eastern Indian state of Assam, and Buddhists of Burmese affiliation in the eastern part of Arunachal Pradesh.
- In Vietnam, geographically part of the region, where historically Theravāda had some presence, especially in the south. The country moreover expanded into Khmer areas with Cambodian Theravāda traditions from the fifteenth century. In the twentieth century, Theravāda gained support amongst ethnic Vietnamese, while Theravāda Buddhists from Vietnam helped to renew the ordination lineage in Cambodia after the Khmer Rouge were defeated.

BURMA

In the region of present-day Burma, Buddhism's first introduction is attributed to an Aśokan mission in the third century BCE. It is possible that this occurred, and there could well have been some Buddhist presence in the following centuries, although it is only from around the third century CE that archaeological evidence is found for Buddhism in the area we now call Burma and Thailand. Early transmissions might have been from India or Sri Lanka; later, interchange with Sri Lanka was important. Perhaps not so very unlike Sri Lanka, varied Indian religious traditions were represented in the first millennium, including Vaiṣṇavite Hinduism, Sarvāstivāda, Mahāyāna, and a form of Buddhism using Pāli. Later, tantric traditions were also present. An eleventh-century Burmese king, however, promoted Theravāda Buddhism, and this marked the beginning of its dominance. Many temples were destroyed during the Mongol invasion in the thirteenth century. Despite an unsettled political history over the following centuries, Buddhism survived. During the second part of the nineteenth century, the penultimate Burmese king, ruling upper Burma, organised an editorial revision of the Pāli Canon. Not long afterwards, Burma became part of the British Indian empire and Buddhism faced similar challenges to those in Sri Lanka.

THAILAND

The Mons who inhabited much of Thailand and southern Burma before the ancestors of the Burmese and Thais moved south into the area, integrated Indian traditions including Hinduism and Buddhism into their cultural life. The Mon kingdom centred in Thailand between the sixth and eleventh centuries CE supported Theravāda Buddhism, and this heritage was taken up by their political successors, including the Burmese kingdom which captured their sacred Pāli texts. There were also other religious strands: the Khmers of Cambodia, whose kingdom was a dominant force in the region between the eighth and fifteenth centuries, supported Hindu and Mahāyāna Buddhist practice, and this had some impact especially between the eleventh and thirteenth centuries when Thailand came under the Khmer state. The Sukhotai kingdom, however, made Theravāda the state religion in the late thirteenth century with the help of Sinhalese monks. In the fourteenth century, also, monks were invited from Sri Lanka to purify the Thai Sangha. The Thai kingdom based at Ayudhya in the following centuries also patronised Theravāda Buddhism and in the eighteenth century, as we have seen, Thai monks were officially invited to Sri Lanka to re-introduce the ordination lineage. In the late eighteenth and nineteenth centuries, the rulers took part in modernising and reforming the Sangha, and the State and religion became more closely linked than ever. Unlike Sri Lanka and Burma, Thailand did not fall to a Western colonial power.

CAMBODIA AND LAOS

The Hindu-Mahāyāna Buddhist ideology of the powerful Khmer kingdom of Cambodia (see above) was officially displaced by Theravāda Buddhism in the fourteenth century. Theravāda seems to have become established beyond the court before the king took it up. Close links with the Thai Sangha were maintained, including reform introduced on the Thai model in the nineteenth century. The area of Laos, which had been part of the Thai Sukhotai kingdom, established its own kingdom in the fourteenth century, with Theravāda as the State religion. Close to Vietnam and China, Mahāyāna Buddhism has also been present as a minority religion. Both Cambodia and Laos came under French colonial administration. In the latter part of the twentieth century, Communist governments created great difficulties for Buddhism in both countries, but there has been some re-building in recent years.

NORTHERN BUDDHISM: TIBET, THE HIMALAYAN AREAS, MONGOLIA, BURYATIA, KALMYKIA AND TUVA

Northern Buddhism refers to the Buddhist traditions deriving from Buddhist transmissions to the Tibetan-speaking areas. Buddhism came to Tibet at the time of the Tibetan empire, between the seventh to ninth centuries, when the Tibetan kingdom entered the international world. Literate culture, including Buddhism, was introduced from India, Central Asia and China, with Imperial funding. Monasteries were founded and translation teams worked on Buddhist texts, including vinaya texts and Mahāyāna literature. In time, it was decided to privilege the transmissions from India. It seems that only limited tantric materials were translated and were kept under tight control. However, after the empire collapsed, tantric Buddhism began to penetrate the culture. From the eleventh century, further waves of Mahāyāna and tantric texts and commentaries were brought from India, from the monastic universities of the Pāla dynasty of Bengal and from wandering tantric teachers. In an environment without a strong centralised state, lamas (Buddhist teachers, mostly but not always monks) and monasteries became economically strong and important for mediating disputes and acting as local power bases.

Although only the Mūlasarvāstivāda's lineage of monastic ordination was represented, monasteries were founded on the basis of affiliation to separate tantric transmissions from India and, in some cases, on the basis of new presentations on the part of an influential lama of the tradition. Only monasteries of the same lineages were organisationally integrated. Even in these cases, daughter monasteries might break away from mother monasteries in time, especially if their lamas came to specialise in different tantric lineages. There was never a single hierarchical structure, but some of the monastic orders were better integrated than others, and there might be links between monasteries in different areas and also teacher–student relations between lamas of different schools.

In the thirteenth century, a Tibetan lama of the Sa-skya school submitted on behalf of the Tibetans to the Mongol armies threatening invasion, after which Tibet became part of the Mongol (Yuan) Chinese empire, and the Sa-skya monastic order became politically dominant in Tibet. A century later, Tibetans regained independence, but a pattern of close connections between aristocratic and monastic authorities continued over the following centuries, while there was variation in which monastic tradition had dominance, and also in the extent of the central government's authority. Large areas in the east were often beyond either the Tibetan or Chinese Government's control and had their own local rulers or a decentralised political structure. From the seventeenth century, the dGe-lugs order gained political supremacy in Central Tibet, and in the mid-eighteenth century, a theocratic form of government was developed with the Dalai Lama as Head of State. The Tibetan State became a Manchu protectorate, but declared its independence in the early twentieth century when the Chinese replaced the Manchu (Qing) dynasty with a Republic. The Chinese invasion in 1951 and the full integration of Tibet into the People's Republic of China after the Tibetan uprising of 1959, when the Dalai Lama along with around 100,000 refugees escaped from Tibet, began a difficult period for Tibetan Buddhism which continues today.

The dGe-lugs-pa developed a rather more integrated monastic system during its centuries in power, with its three monastic centres in the area of the capital, Lhasa, drawing students from monasteries throughout and beyond Tibet itself. The three monasteries wielded considerable power, and monk officials for the Government bureaucracy were also recruited from the dGe-lugs order. However, there were also internal rivalries between the three seats and even between their constituent colleges, as well as between the Lhasa establishment and Tashi Lhunpo, the seat of the Panchen Lama, who was a prominent dGe-lugs lama.

Despite dGe-lugs dominance in Central Tibet, other Buddhist traditions continued to thrive, often having their own local bases, such as the Sa-skya area and the seat of the Karmapa lamas, Tshurpu, in Central Tibet. In the east and in the Himalayan areas outside the Tibetan State's control, non-dGe-lugs monasteries often played a part in political administration.

Like Southern Buddhism, monasteries have been central in Northern Buddhist contexts. It would appear that much larger percentages of the male population became monks in Tibet than is usual in South and South-east Asia, although the South-east Asian practice of temporary monasticism is not found in Tibet. However, the continued existence of monasteries of different schools contrasts in some respects with the slightly more integrated national Sanghas of the Southern Buddhist countries.

Throughout the region, there is much in common in terms of monastic practice and the Mahāyāna bodhisattva training, and all schools have advanced tantric practices. However, there are considerable differences in tantric specialisms and in the scholarly and philosophical interpretations favoured. Although all schools accept the general canonical collections which were made from the fourteenth century (see Chapter 3), the rNying-ma-pa, who follow the transmissions dating back before the 'later diffusion' of texts brought from India from the eleventh century, also have their own, *Ancient Tantra Collection*. Alongside the transmission of old traditions, there are also possibilities for meditative innovation. In the rNying-ma tradition, this includes recognised methods for revealing new scriptures. Other traditions are reluctant to add to the canonical collections, but may nonetheless institutionalise the teaching and transmission of meditative revelations of their principal lamas and, in some cases, they hold the rNying-ma revelations in high regard.

The diversity of practice and doctrine in different schools did not generally translate into separate social groups or sects for a number of reasons:

- Lay communities did not always have exclusive affiliation to one monastic school, and would often sponsor more than one, perform pilgrimage to holy sites associated with famous lamas of different lineages, and receive teachings and blessings from renowned lamas visiting the regional monastic centres of different schools. A family might have one son recruited into a Government-

supported dGe-lugs monastery and another at a local monastery
of a different tradition.

- Lamas would usually have some links with teachers of other
traditions, sometimes receiving part of their training at a monastic college of a different order, or receiving special tantric
transmissions from a lama whose school specialised in the practice. In some cases, a lama's personal 'root teacher' might even
come from a different tradition.
- Lower status monks and tantric practitioners might also receive
teachings at monasteries of different schools.

EASTERN AND NORTH-EASTERN TIBET: KHAM AND AMDO

These areas were ethnically Tibetan and had at times been included
in Tibet when the Tibetan state was strong, such as in the Imperial
era and during the reign of the Fifth Dalai Lama in the seventeenth
century. Much of the region was claimed by China in the early
twentieth century, even if in practice it remained autonomous
until occupied by the Chinese forces in 1949–51. Although the
area might appear politically marginal on the boundaries of the two
states, it was not marginal from the viewpoint of religious history.
After the collapse of the Tibetan empire, the ordination lineage
was apparently maintained in the east. Amdo in the north-east
was not far from the multiethnic centres along the international
trade routes. Eleventh–century Chinese sources seem to indicate a
thriving Tibetan Buddhist culture emerging with monks taking
active political roles. In later times, Amdo became a centre both
of dGe-lugs monasticism and rNying-ma mantra practitioner settlements. A primarily pastoral nomadic region, political organisation was often small scale, with feuds between groups mediated
by the lamas. Kham had its local kingdoms, of which the kingdom of
Dergé (sDe-dge) became the centre of a major ecumenical
movement in the nineteenth century, which still impacts on Tibetan
Buddhism today.

THE HIMALAYAN AREAS: LADAKH, SIKKIM, BHUTAN AND NEPAL

Some Himalayan areas had been in the forefront of the penetration
of Buddhism into Tibet. Ladakh, for instance, was closely connected

to the western Tibetan kingdom of Gu-ge, a major centre for initiating the 'second diffusion' of Buddhism from India in the tenth to eleventh centuries. Important monasteries were established in Ladakh at this time. Himalayan sites became pilgrimage places associated with historic events from Imperial times, although, in some cases, the associations may have been constructed later. The regions also had later waves of Tibetan settlers who brought Tibetan Buddhism with them. Often, ethnic Tibetans lived alongside other Himalayan peoples and, in some cases, adopted some of their cultural traditions. Ladakh is now part of India but, historically, had its own kingdom until 1834. The dGe-lugs and the 'Brug-pa schools established monasteries in Ladakh, while another branch of the 'Brug-pa school moved into Bhutan. Sikkim and Bhutan were established as Tibetan Buddhist states in the seventeenth century. In both cases, Tibetan Buddhists had penetrated the areas a good deal earlier. The kingdoms represented rNying-ma and 'Brug-pa traditions, respectively, at a time when the dGe-lugs-pa were establishing control in Tibet. Sikkim is now within India, while Bhutan remains independent. Other highland areas along the Himalayan ranges also saw an influx of Tibetans at various times. The Sherpas of Nepal, for example, apparently migrated from Kham, establishing themselves in the Solu-Khumbu area by the sixteenth century. They follow rNying-ma practices, and had mainly mantra practitioner traditions with small temples, although monasticism has increased in the modern period. Buddhists of Tibetan ethnicity also live in the Indian state of Arunachal Pradesh, and have been closely connected with neighbouring areas of Tibet and Bhutan.

MONGOLIAN AREAS: MONGOLIA, BURYATIA, KALMYKIA AND TUVA

Central Asian Buddhism along the Silk route had some historical penetration into Mongolian areas in the early centuries CE. In the thirteenth century, the Sa-skya lama became a chaplain to the Mongol court, establishing a pattern of political and religious patronage which was taken up by later Mongol groups in their relations with Tibetan lamas. Contacts between Mongol leaders and Tibetans in the sixteenth to seventeenth centuries led to the far-reaching spread of Tibetan Buddhism amongst Mongol groups, the establishment of monasteries and translation of many Tibetan texts. The fifth Dalai Lama, whose previous incarnation had been a Mongol, founded the Tibetan dGe-lugs-pa State in the seventeenth century with the help of the Gushri Khan (of the Oriat Mongols, whose descendants are now found in Kalmykia). From this period, dGe-lugs Buddhism became the dominant Mongolian Buddhist tradition. The Manchu (Qing) emperors of China continued the promotion of dGe-lugs tradition, and in the eighteenth century, distributed copies of a revised Mongolian edition of the Tibetan canonical texts to many monasteries. Buddhism in Mongolian regions coexisted with the indigenous shamanic traditions, although at times was in conflict with them. As in Tibet, there were large monastic establishments with great economic power and authority until modern times. The seat of the preeminent lama, the Jebtsundamba Khutuktu, was Urga, now Ulaanbaatar, the capital of Mongolia. The Turko-Mongol people of Tuva, now a Republic of Russia, situated in southern Siberia, had been part of the Mongol and Manchu empires. They received Buddhism from Mongolia and were integrated into the Mongolian religious hierarchy. In contrast, the Russian tsar became involved with the Buryat and Kalmyk Buddhist traditions, which became independent of the Mongolian religious structure. In the twentieth century, Buddhism was severely affected by Soviet suppression throughout the areas of Mongolia, Buryatia, Kalmykia, and Tuva, and later by the Cultural Revolution in the region of Inner Mongolia where the population lives under Chinese rule. Fewer Mongolians now live in Inner Mongolia than in Beijing.

EAST ASIAN BUDDHISM: CHINA, TAIWAN, KOREA, VIETNAM AND JAPAN

The first significant transmissions of Buddhism to China date from the Han dynasty during the early centuries of the Christian era. As noted above, the Kuṣāṇa rulers in Central Asia had enthusiastically promoted the establishment and spread of Buddhism, and the Chinese exposure to Buddhism was not only brought about by trade but also by Chinese political and military interests in the Central Asian city states. The Silk route remained central for the transmission of Buddhism to China throughout the first millennium. Buddhism also came to China by sea. Sea trade with South Asia helped to establish early Buddhist centres in southern China in the second to third centuries CE and connections continued in later centuries, although this route was less significant than the Silk road.

In the early period, there were significant developments, such as translations of early Mahāyāna scriptures, although Buddhism remained a small minority interest. The State ideology of Confucianism did not fit well with Buddhism's endorsement of renunciation. An uneasy relationship between Buddhism and the State has been a recurring feature in China. Similar to Tibet in later centuries, however, Buddhism made real inroads into Chinese society during a period without strong centralised government (*the period of disunity*, 311–589). Monasteries had the opportunity to become established, especially in the north where foreign rulers supported Buddhism. Translation work proceeded apace, and particularly in the south which was further away from Central Asian contact, creative adaptations allowed for the development of Buddhist practice and doctrine which harmonised with Chinese cultural traditions of Daoism and Confucianism.

Buddhism became very powerful by the time the Chinese State was reunified under the Sui and then the Tang dynasties (589–906). There were extensive monastic establishments, often with State patronage, which also brought some measure of State control. There were periodic difficulties in relations between Buddhist monks and the State, however, and there were several State persecutions of Buddhism. The most serious in 845 resulted in large-scale destruction of monasteries, the loss of monastic landholdings and the disbanding of a significant proportion of monastics. There was a further State persecution in 955. Nonetheless, despite such troubles, Buddhist monasteries continued to win considerable patronage.

Over the centuries, a full range of texts representing early and Mahāyāna Buddhist traditions were translated, and in the eighth century, early tantric Buddhist traditions as well. The Chinese received the different traditions in numerous separate waves. The same texts – or different expanded version of the same texts – might be translated more than once. Early translations made much use of Daoist vocabulary, while later translations created new Chinese equivalents for the original terms.

In later centuries, the Buddhist traditions co-existed with Confucianism and Daoism with some division of labour but without the kind of privileging of Buddhism which is found in Northern and Southern Buddhist countries. The State varied in attitude towards Buddhist traditions. The early Song dynasty (960–1279) sponsored the first printing of the entire Chinese Buddhist canon (see Chapter 3) and there was some imperial support for Buddhist monasteries during the era, especially those of the Chan tradition. Greater institutionalised State control and a neo-Confucian bureaucracy brought challenges, but Buddhism adapted and thrived. It was the Song period in which the Chinese Buddhist schools took their distinctive shape.

Some of the early Chinese Buddhist schools were based on Indian Buddhist philosophical schools. Later schools were creative developments reflecting the Chinese context. Tiantai traces its origins to the sixth century. It became one of the leading Chinese schools with large numbers of monks and monasteries. It synthesised and hierarchically ordered the teachings of different streams, putting the *Lotus Sūtra* and the Mahāyāna *Mahāparinirvāṇa Sūtra* at the apex. The Huayan school, whose philosophical position arose out of the vision of interpenetrating phenomena conjured up by the *Avataṃsaka Sūtra*, developed from the seventh century. It similarly integrated the teachings of different Buddhist perspectives in a hierarchical list, including the Tiantai, but classing the inter-penetration doctrine as the highest. Both these schools had an impact on later East Asian schools, although they became less significant as separate schools in later centuries.

The Pure Land (Jingtu) school, with a focus on worshipping Amitābha Buddha, traces itself to the sixth century. In the Song period, it penetrated all levels of society, with the creation of lay-controlled associations.

Chan's characteristic practices and sense of its own identity as a school coalesced during the Song. It was divided into a number of groups, although it developed a mythology of its descent from a single earlier lineage. Emphasising meditation rather than study, it necessitated demanding immersion in disciplined practice and made use of Mahāyāna sūtras.

The Mongol Yuan dynasty (thirteenth to fourteenth centuries) led to the introduction of Tibetan tantric traditions, which were also favoured much later by the Manchu Qing dynasty (seventeenth to early twentieth centuries). The Ming dynasty (fourteenth to seventeenth centuries), however, gave some support to Pure Land and Chan. A millenarian theistic rebellion in southern China in the mid-nineteenth century brought destruction to Buddhist temples, necessitating the help of Japanese Buddhists to renew the tradition. The twentieth century was even more difficult for Buddhism in China, especially after the Communist Revolution in 1949 and during the period of the Cultural Revolution (1966–76).

CHINESE MIGRANT COMMUNITIES

Over several hundred years, groups of Chinese migrants have become established in many Asian countries beyond China, such as Malaysia, Singapore, Indonesia and to some extent in Thailand. While developing distinct identities within their host countries, they have often retained Chinese cultural traditions, including Buddhism. These groups, along with Chinese areas outside China's political control, such as Hong Kong until recently, avoided the destruction of the Cultural Revolution, and some have sponsored contemporary Buddhist projects from a position of economic strength.

TAIWAN

Chinese migrants brought Buddhism to Taiwan, especially from the late seventeenth century after the Dutch colonial rulers had been expelled and the Qing took control. Taiwan was brought under Japanese rule from the late nineteenth century until the end of World War II, during which time Japanese forms of Buddhism were promoted. After the War, there was an influx of mainland Buddhist monks. Although Taiwan was spared the excesses of the mainland's Cultural Revolution, the Government kept a tight control over Buddhism until the final decade of the twentieth century. In recent times, there has been considerable growth in Buddhist temples and organisations of various traditions.

KOREA

Buddhism was brought to Korea during the late fourth century, when it was flourishing in China. The introduction into the three Korean kingdoms was connected with the introduction of other elements of Chinese civilisation, such as the Chinese script and literature. Buddhism blended with the indigenous spirit religion and gradually became rooted. After the three kingdoms were unified, Buddhism became very strong in the Unified Shilla period (668–935), and the main Buddhist temples were erected. A number of different schools were established, partly on the basis of the different strands of Chinese Buddhism. Buddhism remained the national religion in the following Koryo Dynasty (935–1392). The school which became the largest Korean Buddhist tradition, the Chogye, had its beginnings in this time, growing out of Korean Chan (Korean *Sŏn*) lineages. However, Buddhism suffered persecution during the Choson Dynasty (1392–1910), when the State became Neo-Confucianist, although many people still remained Buddhist. As in Taiwan, the Japanese occupation meant further difficulties for Korean Buddhism, although there has been Buddhist revival in Post-War South Korea. In North Korea, religion is severely restricted.

VIETNAM

In the early centuries CE, Vietnam was on the route of Buddhist missions from South Asia to China, and Buddhist centres were established there. As an outpost of China, North Vietnam was exposed to Buddhist influences in the first millennium CE, but Buddhism was often linked with unpopular Chinese rule. It became more central after Vietnamese independence in the tenth century, receiving State support and becoming established amongst the people. As in China, it mixed with Daoist and Confucian traditions. From the late fourteenth century, it lost its State position to Confucianism and was at times persecuted or rigidly controlled. Buddhism nonetheless grew in the seventeenth to eighteenth century, when restoration of Buddhist and Daoist temples was sponsored by the Trinh Dynasty. Buddhism played some part in nationalist resistance to French colonial rule, but in the latter part of the twentieth century Buddhism was badly affected by war and Communist government.

As we have seen above, Theravāda has also been found in the south due to Vietnam's proximity to the Southern Buddhist countries, and has gained ground in recent times.

Japan first received its Buddhism from Korean monks in the sixth century, although most of the important traditions in Japan were established later through direct links with China. Initially, Buddhism gained some royal patronage and became established in the area of the capital. By the Nara period (710–94), there were six Buddhist schools, which represented various Buddhist philosophical approaches rather than organisationally distinct sects. Kegon, based on Chinese Huayan (see above), was the most prominent. As in other East Asian contexts, Buddhism began to mix with non-Buddhist elements, from both Daoism and Japanese Shintō, increasing its popular appeal.

The Heian period (794–1185) saw Buddhism at the height of its power and creativity. At the beginning of the period, Tiantai was introduced from China, becoming the Tendai school, which also incorporated the tantric Buddhism of the *Mahāvairocana Tantra*. Chinese tantric lineages also became the basis of the Shingon school, which dates from this time. Shingon has continued to preserve these traditions which later declined in China.

The three traditions that have had most long-term impact were founded in the Kamakura period (1185–1333). Pure Land was developed in the twelfth to thirteenth centuries, inspired by Chinese Pure Land works. Dividing into two branches in Japan, the Jōdo shū (*Pure Land*) and the Jōdo Shinshū (*True Pure Land*) schools, Pure Land became the most popular tradition. As in China, it appealed to ordinary lay devotees.

The two main branches of the Zen (= Chinese Chan) tradition were introduced from China in the same period. Sōtō Zen emphasised sitting meditation in secluded retreats, becoming popular in provincial areas, in part due to the development of funeral services for lay people. Rinzai Zen became more rooted in the seats of power and involved with aristocratic culture such as calligraphy and martial arts. Its meditation practice is similar to Sōtō Zen's but with greater use of *kōan*s or riddles for contemplation which lack straightforward answers.

A number of schools derived from the teachings of the thirteenth-century Nichiren. Like Pure Land, Nichiren Buddhism focuses on a simple practice, in this case, the recitation of the title of the Lotus

Sūtra, which is the tradition's main scriptural source, supplemented by the works of Nichiren.

Buddhism continued to thrive although it became increasingly bureaucratised and subject to State control in the Edo period (1603–1867). The Meiji Restoration (1868) brought an enforced separation of Buddhism and Shintō, and ended the requirement of celibacy for the clergy, as mentioned in Chapter 4. After a difficult period for Buddhism under the twentieth-century militaristic Empire, there has been some revival of the traditional Buddhist groups and new Buddhist movements in the Post-War period.

BUDDHIST TRADITIONS TODAY: SOME MAJOR THEMES

MODERNISATION AND POLITICAL TRANSFORMATIONS IN ASIAN COUNTRIES

Buddhism has suffered great setbacks in the past two hundred years, measured in terms of the number of active monasteries and monastics, the extent of monastic land-holdings, State support, monastic influence over education and the integration of Buddhism and local socio-cultural identities. In part, these changes have been connected with socioeconomic modernisation, and similar to changes in the position of Christian churches in Western countries. In Asia, how-ever, they have frequently been linked to colonial subjection, to political upheaval and to direct attacks on Buddhism by Communist governments.

The most significant structural changes have been changes either in the political and economic system as such or in the level of control exercised by the State over religious institutions, coupled with the State take-over of social and economic functions formerly provided by monasteries. While there are significant differences in the rate and type of political change in various Asian countries, all without exception had been affected by political modernisation processes long before the advance of Communism. Even Tibet's premodern ecclesiastical state, often misleadingly seen as a survival of a medieval system, had undergone transformation over several hundred years. The political structure of the Dalai Lama's government which dates from the mid-eighteenth century created a bureaucracy in which even the monk officials became in effect life-long career bureaucrats. They answered to the State administration rather than to their monasteries to whom they might have little more than nominal affiliation. The monasteries with their landed estates continued to carry great weight but various moves towards further modernisation in the nineteenth and early twentieth century had been changing the balance of power in favour of the State. Large monastic estates came to have less autonomy by the twentieth century than they had once enjoyed. The State encroached also on areas which had formerly been the preserve of monasteries. One example is the early twentieth-century foundation of a new State-supported college of traditional medicine, which recruited from the laity as well as from monasteries, and provided an alternative to the monastic colleges.

In several other Asian countries, the monasteries were subjected to greater State control. In Thailand, where the Buddhist monastic hierarchy was already more centralised, nineteenth-century reforms of the monastic discipline and curriculum were State sponsored, and the new system was also taken up by the Cambodian State. Where Asian countries were brought under Western Colonial authorities, such as in Sri Lanka and Burma, disestablishment had a rather different impact, including some element of independence for monasteries from direct State interference. Nonetheless, it also served to restrict the scope for Buddhist monastic institutions to represent a relatively autonomous structure of authority with real influence on the society. Outright dismantling of Buddhist monasticism by the State had been witnessed for a brief period in the late nineteenth century in Japan, as we have seen in Chapter 4. Such measures were more profound and long-standing in the twentieth century in countries under Communist rule, including Mongolian areas under the USSR in the early to mid-twentieth century, areas of China, Inner Mongolia and Tibet under the People's Republic of China (PRC) in the mid to late twentieth century, and South-east Asian countries such as Vietnam and Cambodia in the late twentieth century. But almost everywhere, political modernisation has either resulted in greater State control over the Buddhist Sangha in comparison with the historical past, or the curtailing or abolition of its formal role in Asian polities, or both, especially in the case of Communist States.

Socioeconomic change has gone hand in hand with the structural political changes. Besides land reform breaking up monastic estates, modern economic developments bringing modern forms of production and urbanisation have undermined the centrality of Buddhist monasteries within Asian communities. The kind of situation discussed in Chapter 4, of monasteries with landed estates, recruiting from the local community and integrally related to it, perhaps having some role in arbitration of disputes, in education, or in other social affairs, may persist in some areas of Asia but not in an entirely unchanged form. For instance, the simple expansion of the role of the State in provision of education and social services in Buddhist majority countries has not only created opportunities in secular education and training, of greater relevance in today's economy, but undermined monastic monopolies even over the teaching of Buddhism itself.

Just as Christianity and Judaism in the West have had to adapt to more secularised social structures, the dominance of scientific and technological systems of knowledge, and socio-cultural pluralism, so religions in Asia have also had to make similar adjustments, often in a rather more dramatic or sudden manner. It was, moreover, not only the monastic structures which came under attack in Communist countries. Individual religious belief and practice was systematically targeted during the Cultural Revolution in China, and remains under State scrutiny and restraint in many areas in the PRC. Throughout Asia, not only have some Buddhist beliefs been challenged indirectly by the advance of modern scientific knowledge, but full training in Buddhist philosophy and practices seems less viable in modern societies. As we have seen, Buddhist religious and meditative knowledge was sustained by community commitment to the support of monastic specialists and monastic institutions. With less social investment in religious expertise, individual choice to undergo such training requires greater personal commitment at a time when more secular opportunities may be available.

NEW ROLES FOR BUDDHIST MONKS AND MONASTERIES IN MODERN ASIAN SOCIETIES

Although the dramatic social structural changes in Asia in the past century have severely curtailed 'traditional' Buddhist organisation,

Buddhism has also undergone adaptations which have meant that Buddhist monasteries have in many areas remained viable institutions into the twenty-first century. One kind of adaptation has been new kinds of social involvements for monasteries. In some ways, monastic involvement in rural development projects or environmental protection, as seen in parts of South-east Asia, might be considered a radical departure from the monastic code which enjoins monks to avoid worldly involvements. Yet, we have also noted that pre-modern monastic organisation embroiled monastic establishments in political and economic affairs, even if large numbers of resident monks might be entirely occupied with their religious pursuits. New interpretations of traditional Buddhist virtues, such as loving kindness and the protection of living beings, have helped to bring acceptance of such new kinds of responsibilities, sometimes even in rather conservative monastic traditions. For instance, some Thai Theravāda 'Forest Monks' who emphasise a strict adherence to the monastic code have, since the late 1980s, taken on responsibilities for protecting the trees in the areas of their forest homes and discouraging deforestation.

There have also been modern style movements, such as the international 'Engaged Buddhism' promoted by the Vietnamese monk Thich Nhat Hanh, developed initially out of an attempt to provide a modern Buddhist way for seeking reconciliation, peace and social justice in the polarised and devastating circumstances of 1960s Vietnam. Another example is Santi Asoke, a new Buddhist movement in Thailand which was required to separate itself from the established Sangha, and which has mixed communities of monastics and lay people living together. With a reformist message, it promotes a simple anti-materialistic lifestyle in line with Buddhist morality, including vegetarianism, together with socially useful work.

POLITICAL ACTIVISM AND MORAL DILEMMAS IN BUDDHIST CONTEXTS

Perhaps the most striking and controversial of present-day adaptations of the traditional political involvement of Buddhist monasteries has been the engagement in Buddhist nationalism, political resistance and ethnic defence. In the development of modern nation states in Asia, Buddhism has frequently been taken up by rulers and politicians as one way of unifying socially disparate groups and to forge a sense of a single cultural and national identity. This is one reason why modernising governments have sought to centralise and to increase control over their country's monastic institutions. To some extent, we find continuity with the pre-modern pattern of the Buddhist order patronised by and legitimating the king who rules in accordance with the Buddhist Dharma. But with the political upheavals of the past centuries, the Buddhist monastic order has not always simply accepted the status quo. In cases of colonial occupation, both under Western and other Asian powers, such as the Chinese occupation of Tibet, Buddhism became important in nationalist and ethnic resistance. Buddhist monks and nuns have often been at the forefront of such resistance. A similar pattern has also been a feature of political protest under oppressive regimes. Thus, in Burma in the late twentieth and early twenty-first century, the opposition has combined calls for democracy with traditional Buddhist virtues and monks have joined protests.

The involvement of monks and monastic institutions in such political action nonetheless remains deeply controversial for two reasons which are universally applicable in Asian Buddhist contexts, apart from any particular regional issues. First, participation in political conflict would seem to go against the spirit of the vinaya code and social expectations of seemly behaviour for monastics, which in political contexts might be rather the role of peace-makers or moral advisors to politicians and rulers. When political confrontation leads to violence, it brings into question the compatibility of the monks' practice with a discipline based on the first precept of not taking life. There have been many examples in the historical past in which Buddhists and Buddhist monasteries have supported violent political action for what they perceived to be the long-term good of the Buddhist Dharma and community. The construction of Buddhism as consistently non-violent is not misleading as a perennial ideal, but social realities have often meant that the practice has not always matched the ideals.

In the contemporary world, the moral high ground may be fiercely contested. One approach, witnessed in some of the small yet often influential ascetic monk traditions, upholds an uncompromising commitment to renunciation of all political involvements as antithetical to real spiritual development. In contrast, an active engagement with political concerns which still maintains adherence to traditional Buddhist virtues, thus seeking to promote social justice through dialogue and peace-making efforts, may resonate with many in today's Asian Buddhist communities. Indeed, two important figures in Asian politics today, the Dalai Lama of Tibet and Aung San Suu Kyi of Burma, could be said to represent this position, and have gained international respect and support for their efforts to find resolution to their people's problems by combining traditional Buddhist ethics with commitment to modern principles of democracy, human rights and social justice. However, in a world where non-violence and appeasement appears to have little impact on those wielding political power, we cannot be surprised that more radical alternatives of support for direct confrontation and even armed struggle may seem preferable to a significant group of people, justifiable as a desperate attempt to recreate the viability of their Buddhist communities today.

A second reason for controversy over political activism concerns another of Buddhism's ethical principles, its universalism. This comes to the fore especially in cases where Buddhism is adopted as a symbolic identity marker of a specific group. If Buddhism is associated with one nation or ethnic group in contrast to another, this may not fit altogether comfortably with Buddhism's universalistic claims. The problem would seem especially stark in the Sri Lankan example where there has been conflict between the majority Sinhalese Buddhist community and the minority Tamils, most of whom are Hindus. Buddhist nationalism had become a real political force during the struggle with the colonial British Government and has remained strong since Independence. Yet an identification between Buddhist and national identity would seem problematic in the light of non-Buddhist minorities (including Catholics and Muslims in some areas) and especially when Buddhist nationalism is brought into conflict with Tamils seeking their own political autonomy. In this case, important factions of the Buddhist order have been in the vanguard of an exclusivist and aggressive nationalism. But more moderate voices have also carried the moral weight of probably greater consistency with Buddhist values.

Similar considerations also have relevance in the case of Tibetan nationalism. A common Buddhist identity has helped to unify ethnic Tibetans from different areas within the PRC. Tibetan determination to re-build their cultural heritage, devastated by the Chinese invasion and integration into the PRC, has seen astonishing results in the impressive re-construction of Buddhist monasteries and temples in Tibet and in exile in India and the Himalayan countries. An opposition between Tibetan Buddhism and the Chinese State was ironically intensified by the Chinese Communist persecution of Buddhism. Rather like the strength of Catholicism in Poland during the period of Communist rule, continued restrictions on Buddhist practice if anything hardens Tibetan resolve to support it. Yet the growth in Tibetan Buddhist nationalism may seem slightly paradoxical when many Chinese are Buddhists, and increasingly in the contemporary world, the followings of Tibetan lamas often include Chinese adherents. This has at times been uncomfortable for the Chinese State as also for Tibetan freedom movements. The Dalai Lama has, with varying degrees of success, sought to divorce the Tibetan struggle for autonomy and social justice from a narrow Tibetan nationalism, explicitly trying to make links with Chinese Buddhists and dissidents supporting a move to democracy in the PRC.

It is clear that there is not a simple 'Buddhist position' which has dominated relations between politics and religion in Buddhist majority countries in contemporary Asia. But it is also clear that Buddhism continues to be a significant factor in political and social life, despite the losses to the Buddhist monastic establishment brought about by modernisation and twentieth-century conflicts.

THE IMPACT OF POSTMODERNITY

Social scientists speak of a development from the conditions of *modernity* to contemporary *postmodernity*, or an alternative contrast between *early* and *late modernity*. To simplify the debate and disregard disagreements between the characterisation of these stages, early *modernity* may be said to be marked, for instance, by the dominance of State and rational bureaucratic structures in many areas of social life, by industrial production, and by the dominance of positivist science, rationality, and ideas of progress towards a better and more socially just world. In Buddhist contexts, imperatives for reform, an interest in recovering the Buddha's 'original' message as defined by the early texts instead of traditional authorities, and a focus on the rational aspects of Buddhist teaching, together with a tendency to downplay the less reasoned mystical or magical elements, have been associated with modernity. These features remain part of many presentations of Buddhism today but they are not always central to the most successful religious organisations.

Today, the promise of rationality taking precedence in the world of international finance or in other areas of social and economic organisation may seem remote – witness, for instance, the events of the 2008 *Credit Crunch*. This is perhaps all the more true in Asian countries which have gone through the political and economic upheavals discussed above. The certainties of early modern scientific advance seem to have given way to uncertainties or the baffling processes at the heart of the discipline of Physics, which may remain rigorously rational to research scientists but suggest irrational mystery to the uninitiated. Other features of *postmodernity* (or *late modernity*) include the development of mass media and consumerism, ethnic and cultural pluralism, as well as the atomisation of social life in the city. Individuals may become unembedded from traditional neighbourhood and kinship groups, perhaps inducing a state of *anomie*, or social isolation and stress, but also reduced social constraints, and the possibility for greater individual choice and experimentation in livelihood and lifestyle, including religion. The development of communications and the internet has enabled viable transnational communities, including religious organisations. Moreover, mass media of television, film and music, and electronic resources and communication, have often privileged visual and auditory modes carrying emotional and symbolic imagery over the rational argument of the carefully-crafted published book which characterised early modernity. Internet resources may encourage individual paths of links through associated materials rather than a logically-ordered linear progression from clear beginnings to conclusions. All this may favour greater variation and rather more expressive and experimental versions of religion than those which were widespread in the past.

In these circumstances, new kinds of religious organisation and approaches to the teaching and practice of Buddhism have taken root in recent times. With traditional monastic establishments less able to control the teaching and practice of Buddhism beyond the monastery gates, there has been more scope for individual monks or small groups to write books, hold public meetings, attract followings and teach in a manner less constrained than that of a traditional monastic setting. Modern urban environments have especially encouraged the development of lay Buddhist associations and an expanded role for lay Buddhists within monastic traditions. There may be a new level of expectation that lay practitioners can and should directly access the meditative and textual training which had once been the exclusive preserve of monastic expertise. The publication of the Pāli Canon and then translations from it in printed books, and widely distributed books about Buddhism from the late nineteenth century meant that those who had a literate education were not so dependent on monks for introduction to Buddhist knowledge and their religious explorations could be more directly tailored to their own interests and choices.

In sociological studies of Christianity it is sometimes suggested that the vitality of Christianity in the USA in modern times in contrast with European countries is at least partly related to the deliberate constitutional separation between Church and State. This freed the Churches from the constraints of establishment and allowed more dynamic organisation, responsive to the community of adherents. Similarly, more recently, Christian evangelical groups throughout the world have been able to spread and grow without the need to negotiate the complex structures of authority which characterise the traditional Churches. Although not directly comparable, the weakening of traditional Buddhist monastic hierarchies in Asia may have helped provide the space for the development of new Buddhist groups, such as the Japan-based international lay Buddhist movement Sōka Gakkai. With a central headquarters in Tokyo and other large centres elsewhere, local affiliated groups are easily set up. They often meet in the homes of supporters, and may be coordinated and expand using social and kinship networks of interested individuals, which may mean that the organisation need not always depend on widespread local community support. Such a structure also provides an environment where their chanting practice, fairly simple by Buddhist standards, is supported by discussion with more experienced and knowledgeable members in a context which allows for the application of the religious teaching to the individual's and local group's own situation. The Dhammakāya Movement, stemming from a Thai meditation master, is another example of an alternative to traditional Buddhist organisation and it has large numbers of monastic and lay followers. It has operated with considerable success, if at times criticised for its fundraising and other unconventional methods. It rejects the standard Theravāda interpretations of the scriptures, and has developed its own ordination procedures and distinctive teachings on uncovering the pure 'dharma body' within each person.

One theme of contemporary applications of Buddhist teachings, especially in modern urban environments, is a tendency for a re-framing of Buddhist practices to address more directly what traditional Buddhism would see as short-term worldly goals. In modern economies, there may be fierce competition for employment and success may seem to depend on a fortuitous combination of circumstances as well as individual application and achievement. The loss of the social support networks of more stable communities may provide further stresses. In such circumstances, those offering to perform rituals to increase wealth, health or fortune may be in high demand. As mentioned in Chapter 4, historical Buddhism has much scope for the provision of services by monks thought to generate merit which can be specifically dedicated for the benefit of an individual or group, say in situations of illness or misfortune, or to increase good fortune. Traditional Buddhist specialists continue to provide services for modern requirements but there may be some distinctive features of the new situation. In Southern Buddhism, traditionally, Pāli verses (*paritta*) may be recited by monks, helping to create well-being, while more explicitly manipulative rituals focusing on local or regional deities and spirits are often the preserve of non-monastic specialists. But in modern towns such as Colombo in Sri Lanka, there has been increased direct involvement by monks in such rituals. For example, monks may now preside over deity shrines which cater for instrumental rites within Buddhist temples.

In other instances, we may see continuity with traditional monastic rituals, such as a case of young Japanese students corresponding with Tibetan exiled monks in India, sponsoring traditional Tibetan Buddhist rites to ensure their exam success. Such rituals represent an extension of traditional services provided by monks for lay people, although the choice of one group of monks rather than another may now have little to do with former long-term relationships between a monastery and its local community. The rites may also be comparatively abbreviated, where in modern life there may not be the time and resources to invest in elaborate ritual performances with all parties present.

One important distinction between traditional monastic ritual and many new versions of Buddhist practices is that the content of the service itself is now more often conceptualised principally in terms of addressing the lay concerns. For instance, monks might recite a holy text, such as the Pāli *Mettā Sutta* (Sn 1.8), the *Discourse on Loving Kindness*, and such recitations may help in cultivating the virtuous qualities the discourse extols as well as engendering merit which may benefit another. Today, however, there is demand for Buddhist practices which can be applied directly by the individual to the problem situation. Meditative and chanting practices may be promoted and taught as a direct means for reducing stress, or for healing, or even for creating worldly success. Such re-interpretations are especially striking in the case of meditation practices designed to engender tranquillity, insight and Enlightenment. Once the pre-serve of an elite of the most dedicated and disciplined monastics, the practices may now be presented as a way for those with health problems to restore their mental or bodily balance. Simplified or specially adapted versions of traditional practices may be used in this way. Of course, presentations geared towards therapy – or perhaps closer to a traditional understanding, as simply engendering a calm state of mind – do not preclude encouragement towards more tra-ditional aims of spiritual development. In some cases, established religious teachers are responsible for adaptations to techniques, which may be taught to their own groups of followers or to much larger audiences through public teachings or books. There may also be a distinction between the versions of the practices taught to mass audiences and more traditional versions retained for an inner circle of committed students. Lay religious associations may also popularise simplified practices.

However, it is important not to overstate the prevalence of instrumental motives in the contemporary context of increased lay participation in Buddhist practice. Another feature of religion today is the growth of interest in spirituality and the search for inner meaning. In fact, even some of the apparently materialistic motiva-tions which characterise contemporary religious explorations might be more appropriately considered as yearning for personal fulfilment and happiness. Buddhism is well placed to cater for such interests. As we have seen, mainstream basic Buddhist teaching begins with a direct experiential analysis of the individual and the world, and encourages individual inner questioning and experimentation to find the truth. Existential suffering is directly addressed in the first Truth (see Chapter 2), and blissful release which it is possible for the individual to realise is at the heart of Buddhist doctrine. Moreover, the investment over centuries in support for contemplative practices has meant that there are a wide range of meditative techniques, of practical manuals for spiritual development and of visionary literature. For those of a more intellectual bent, there are sophisticated philosophical teachings and debate. Early Buddhist teachings often follow through reasoned argument, and may consider the opinions of a wide range of opponents, given that they were developed in a context of rival renouncer groups and brahmanic practice. The implications of the teachings were thrashed out in the philosophy developed in later Buddhist monastic universities, which resulted in a number of different schools of thought. The contemporary 'spiritual marketplace' has meant that, increasingly, there are possibilities for individual spiritual seekers to make their own choices about which religious systems they will sign up to, and Buddhism offers not one but many varieties of spiritual practice and intellectual training.

Today's spiritual seekers may expect a religious path which gives them full access to the religious training yet does not demand the full-time commitment nor the renunciation of worldly pursuits which the traditional contemplative discipline entailed. To cater for such interests, meditation practice or chanting routines may be developed so that sessions can be fitted into a busy work schedule, or regular residential retreats organised for lay people. The apparent discrepancy from a traditional perspective between the religious expectations and the lifestyle need not indicate a consumerist approach that instant Enlightenment can be obtained at little personal cost. In fact, the adaptation of the active lay Buddhist role into one which may involve a considerable investment of 'leisure' time and resources, perhaps as well as continuing the more traditional patronage of monasteries or new style Buddhist centres, may be far from an easy option. And although the social structural reasons mentioned above have contributed to a decline in monastic recruitment, full-time long-term renunciation has not yet been entirely eclipsed. In fact, interest in recovering the ancient heritage of virtuous discipline and in seeking the full Enlightenment extolled in the Buddhist scriptures has encouraged renewed support for reclusive contemplative traditions such as the Theravāda Forest monasteries and Tibetan retreat centres.

THE INTERNATIONALISATION OF BUDDHISM

Globalisation of economic and social organisation has brought with it an unprecedented degree of everyday communications across the world. Even before recent dramatic growth in international links, the past century of Asian political and economic changes brought new patterns of international migration and cultural contact. The Buddhist traditions of different Asian countries have been internationalised in many ways: by the publication of texts and resources in modern books and, more recently, by film, television and the internet; by the settlement of Buddhist migrant communities in different countries; by the long-distance travel of Buddhist teachers and monks to different areas; by international interest generated through media coverage of prominent Buddhist figures; by Buddhist organisations setting out to expand into new areas; and by the interests or study of international visitors to Buddhist countries, from colonial administrators to postmodern spiritual seekers.

Of course, international movement and expansion is hardly new for Buddhism, but the scale, speed and nature of today's openings for communication and missionary activities are of a different order from those of the past. Historical gradual penetrations of a new area through trading activities or an organised establishment of Buddhism by a ruler would seem a quite different model from the typical expansion now, which may owe more to chance connections and contacts, a teacher's charisma, or individual enthusiasms. There are two especially striking features of contemporary expansions of Buddhism. One is the continuous high level of feedback between the tradition and country of origin and the recruits and the wider society of the destination countries. A Buddhist teacher may travel and set up new groups in different countries, returning with new ideas and perhaps adaptations in organisation or religious practices suggested or requested by the new students. Further adjustments might come both ways through continuing electronic communications and visits by students in both directions. A Buddhist centre newly formed by Western convert Buddhists in communication with an Asian teacher or monastery may attract Asian migrant Buddhists, leading to processes of cultural negotiation and adaptation, which, again, may feed back to the organisation's other geographical centres.

A second frequently occurring striking feature is the introduction of more than one different Buddhist tradition and, in some cases, participation in one group of followers of various ethnic or cultural origins. In the Kathmandu valley in Nepal, long-established Newar Buddhist traditions have been joined by a large number of Tibetan monasteries or temples of different schools set up by exiled Tibetan lamas, as well as several Theravāda Buddhist monasteries, mainly with Sri Lankan affiliations but also with some links to Burma and Thailand. Besides the cultural accommodations or new kinds of presentations which the incoming groups may need to make to attract local support for their presence, an important aspect of this kind of scenario – even when the new temples may not make large inroads into traditional affiliations – is that the established tradition may need to become reflexive of its own practice. It may defend its traditions or reform them but, either way, it is unlikely to be entirely unchanged by the encounter, especially if the new groups explicitly challenge the authenticity or basis in Buddhist principles of local tradition, charges which may be more hard-hitting from rival Buddhists rather than other religions. Many Western countries now have a wide variety of Buddhist traditions established in their cities. New recruits may have already explored other Buddhist (and non-Buddhist) traditions and come with a colourful mix of Buddhist, New Age, Christian and local cultural assumptions and practices gathered on the way. And in today's multi-cultural cities, a Tibetan Buddhist group may attract Europeans of different nationalities and backgrounds, over-seas Chinese and Mongolian participants. The newly established groups need to be responsive to their followers' backgrounds, open enough to accommodate their beliefs and requirements, or having carefully developed strategies for persuading their adherents to re-think their former approaches.

Another aspect of increasing awareness of and contact between different Buddhist traditions has been the development of Buddhist ecumenical debate and co-operation, pan-Buddhist organisations, and religious exchanges arranged between monks and teachers of different traditions. 'Sakyadhita', the 'International Association of Buddhist Women' established in 1987, which has encouraged collaboration between Buddhist nuns of different traditions and cross-tradition discussion of the revival of the full nun's ordination, is an example of such a movement. Religious exchanges between traditions may lead to creative adaptations of traditional presentations of teachings. For instance, a Tibetan lama who had studied in Sri Lanka and learnt Pāli, framed a traditional Tibetan presentation in terms of a Pāli classification when teaching a Western Buddhist audience in London who were more familiar with Theravāda teachings.

In general, greater contact between Buddhists of different Asian traditions has not yet fuelled much interest in new mergers. Traditional respect for well-established lineages of practice has persisted even in countries where Buddhism is newly imported, so most Western Buddhists would still see themselves as part of one or another Asian Buddhist tradition. Migrant Asians who often maintain their own community's traditional religious affiliation are at present still a majority of the Buddhists in Western countries. Nonetheless, there have been some new Buddhist groups or movements which have sought to transcend traditional sectarian boundaries. For example, a number of groups are based on the promotion of Theravāda Vipassanā (insight) Meditation, especially as taught by Burmese teachers. The movement of S.N. Goenka (a student of the Burmese Sayagyi U Ba Khin) emphasises that the practice can be done by followers of any religion or none, since the Buddha only taught the Dhamma (Dharma), not any sectarian religion. A group which goes further than this, seeking to establish a new Buddhism which draws upon different Asian traditions and which is specifically Western in orientation, is the Friends of the Western Buddhist Order (FWBO). Based in the UK but now an international group, the FWBO developed a form of lay ordination based on *Going for Refuge* and the lay precepts, and has experimented with community living and cooperative Buddhist businesses. For most Western Buddhists, however, the primary mentors are still Asian, and cultural adjustments are ongoing, such as the balance between using Asian or Western languages in Buddhist chanting and ritual practices.

It can be hard to assess the relative significance of social structural factors and of cultural differences in new characteristics of

Buddhism. For instance, we have seen that declining monastic recruitment might have much to do with modern socioeconomic organisation. In the West, it is often claimed rather to have more to do with Western cultural norms which, especially in historically Protestant countries, do not give high value to, and may even belittle, the status of monks or celibate priests. Thus, even where long-term retreat practice may be entered, Western Buddhists may retain their lay identities. From this perspective, it can even be argued that similar developments in Asian urban contexts have been influenced by Western cultural contacts, such as influencing middle-class Buddhism in Sri Lanka in a 'Protestant' direction. It is impossible to separate out such real life complexities, especially when cultural influences can be reciprocal and developed over time. And it would certainly be a mistake to assume that Asian Buddhists have been at the mercy of a Western 'Orientalism' dominating the cultural exchanges. On the contrary, Asian Buddhists have been the main driving force in contemporary explorations and promotion of new directions for Buddhism in the context of today's socio-political realities.

CHAPTER SUMMARY

- The model of the three major extant regions of Southern, Northern and East Asian Buddhism should not detract us from overlaps and omissions, such as the historical influence of Central Asia.
- In Southern Buddhism, the heritage of Theravāda Buddhism as developed in Sri Lanka has been central although there are varied histories in the different South and South-east Asian countries.
- Northern Buddhism is dominated by Mahāyāna and tantric traditions introduced into and developed in Tibet between the seventh and twelfth centuries, although there are regional diversities in Tibet, the Himalayan and Mongolian areas.
- Mahāyāna transmissions to China, translated into Chinese and later re-formulated by new Chinese Buddhist schools, have been the basis for East Asian Buddhism, which has then been adapted in other East Asian countries.
- Modernisation and socio-political changes have had great impact on the formal organisation of Buddhism, with monasteries losing much of their historical centrality in Asian communities.

- New roles have been found for Buddhist monasteries in modern times and there have been new kinds of political involvements, some controversial.
- Expansion of lay participation has included adjustments to Buddhist practices for lay instrumental purposes and the spiritual search.
- The internationalisation of Buddhism has meant greater contact between different Buddhist traditions and continuing cultural exchanges, encouraging dynamic re-presentations even in the countries of origin as well as in new areas for Buddhism, such as the West.

FURTHER READING

DIFFERENT BUDDHIST TRADITIONS

Bechert, Heinz and Richard Gombrich (eds) 1984 *The World of Buddhism: Buddhist Monks and Nuns in Society and Culture*. Illustrated historical surveys of Buddhism in different Asian countries and a final chapter (Bechert) on 'Buddhist Revival in East and West'.

Harvey, Peter 1990 *An Introduction to Buddhism: Teachings, History and Practices*. Detailed information on the main Buddhist schools and their varied expressions.

Woodhead, Linda, Paul Fletcher, Hiroko Kawanami and David Smith (eds) 2009 *Religions in the Modern World*. The chapter on Buddhism (Cantwell and Kawanami) gives case studies of Tibet and Southeast Asia, while East Asian examples are addressed in the chapters on Chinese Religions (Feuchtwang) and Japanese Religions (Kisala).

STUDIES OF CONTEMPORARY BUDDHISM IN SPECIFIC COUNTRIES

Darlington, Susan M. 2000 'Rethinking Buddhism and Development: The Emergence of Environmentalist Monks in Thailand'.

Goldstein, Melvyn C. and Matthew Kapstein 1998 *Buddhism in Contemporary Tibet*. Collected articles on many aspects of contemporary Tibetan Buddhism.

Gombrich, Richard and Gananath Obeyesekere 1988 *Buddhism Transformed: Religious Change in Sri Lanka*. An exploration of Buddhism in modern Sri Lanka including 'Protestant Buddhism' and Buddhist involvements in deity cults.

Reader, Ian 1991 *Religion in Contemporary Japan*. Includes an interesting description of life in a Soto Zen monastery.

Tambiah, Stanley 1984 *The Buddhist Saints of the Forest and the Cult of Amulets*. A study of Thai Forest monasteries and their charismatic teachers.

INFLUENTIAL BUDDHIST LEADERS TODAY

Aung San Suu Kyi 1995 *Freedom from Fear and Other Writings*.
Dalai Lama, The 1990 *Freedom in Exile: The Autobiography of The Dalai Lama*.
Thich Nhat Hanh 1999 *Interbeing: Fourteen Guidelines for Engaged Buddhism*.

GLOSSARY OF TECHNICAL TERMS

Note that where two forms of a term are given, separated by a slash (/), the first is the Sanskrit and the second the Pāli version of the same word.

Abhidharma

Further or Higher Dharma or teachings, the third section (*basket*) of the threefold division of Buddhist scriptures, containing systematised presentation and analysis of the early doctrine.

Āgama(s)

A class of early Buddhist texts corresponding to the early Pāli suttas, preserved by other early Buddhists, and translated into Chinese.

Arhat/Arahant

An enlightened one whose sense desires, desire for becoming, wrong views and ignorance have been extinguished. This was the ideal in early Buddhism, remaining so in Southern Buddhism, but superseded to some extent in the Mahāyāna traditions by the bodhisattva ideal for buddhahood. Arhats nonetheless continued to be seen as saints in East Asian and Northern Mahāyāna countries.

Bodhisattva/Bodhisatta

A being intent on Enlightenment: a term used for the Buddha before his Enlightenment, and later, especially in the Mahāyāna, any person who aspires for the completely perfected Enlightenment of a Buddha.

Brahmanism

Religious system of the Indian Brahman priests at the time of the Buddha.

Buddha

The Awakened One, who has realised *completely perfected Enlightenment*. It can refer to the historical founder of Buddhism in our world system and also (later) to other Buddhas said to exist in other times and places. It implies the principle of Enlightenment attained by the individual, rather than being a personal name for an individual.

Dependent Arising (Pratītyasamutpāda)

The doctrine concerning the laws governing the causal processes of life, presented as twelve dependent 'links'.

Dhāraṇī

A string of sacred syllables or a text based on such a string, *dhāraṇī* were often used in Mahāyāna sūtras and also formed independent texts which were generally later classified as lower tantra texts. The term is still occasionally used for mantras in later tantric texts although, in the later tantras, the word applies more commonly to the visualised female tantric deity or the yogin's female partner.

Dharma/Dhamma

In Buddhism, Dharma means the Buddha's teachings, the Truth they embody and the path to realise them. It can also be used as a technical term (usually given with a lower case 'd' in English) to mean the fundamental elements of existence.

Dharmakāya

See: Triple Body of the Buddha (three *kāya*s).

Dhyāna/Jhāna
Deep absorptions: specifically, in early Buddhism and in the Theravāda, a set of four meditative states which can serve as a foundation for Enlightenment, as in the descriptions of the Buddha's own Enlightenment and final Nirvāṇa. *Dhyāna* or the deep absorption of a bodhisattva is the fifth item in the list of the six bodhisattva transcendent actions.

Duḥkha/Dukkha
Suffering or unease: a condition characterising worldly life.

Eightfold Path, Noble
The presentation of the Buddhist path, as given in the *Dhammacakkappavattana Sutta* in the Pāli *Saṃyutta Nikāya* collection (which is classified as the Buddha's first discourse).

Enlightenment or Liberation or Realisation
The complete ending of Ignorance and craving, and the attainment of wisdom – the final goal in Buddhism.

Four Truths of the Noble Ones
A teaching on the nature of worldly existence, given in the *Dhammacakkappavattana Sutta* and many other sources. It consists of: (1) the problem – *duḥkha* (suffering or unrest); (2) its cause – *craving*; (3) its cessation – the possibility of liberation by stopping the cause; (4) the Path to the cessation of *duḥkha* – the Noble Eightfold Path.

Ignorance (Avidyā)
Often considered the fundamental cause underlying the conditions of Saṃsāra. An early definition gives it as taking the view that what is in the condition of unrest and suffering is not in this condition, that what is in fact impermanent is permanent, that what lacks 'self' is 'self', and that what is repulsive is delightful.

Jain(s)
A rival śramaṇa movement, Buddhists considered the Jains to practise the 'extreme' of asceticism.

Jātaka

A collection of Buddhist tales, especially concerning the Buddha's previous lives, preserved in the Pāli Canon and similar scriptural collections maintained in other Buddhist traditions.

Jewels

The three Jewels: Buddha, Dharma, Sangha.

Karma(n)/Kamma

In Buddhism, intentional activities that have effects perpetuating worldly existence. The results depend on whether the actions are virtuous or non-virtuous from a Buddhist ethical perspective.

Knowledges, three

The three Knowledges are said to have characterised the Buddha's Enlightenment: (1) direct knowledge of one's previous births; (2) knowledge of the births and deaths of beings, and the causal processes of karma; (3) knowledge of the cessation of craving and ignorance and release from the cycle of rebirth.

Mahāyāna

A movement that emerged in the first century BCE and which recognised new sūtras. Although a minority movement in India, the Mahāyāna was historically important and spread throughout Asia, becoming dominant in Northern and East Asian Buddhism.

Maṇḍala

A tantric sacred circle, used in tantric Buddhism to symbolise the environment transformed into a Buddha field, with its different features expressing and integrating various aspects of enlightened experience. Maṇḍala architectural structures can be used in outer ritual practice, while maṇḍalas may also be used in internal tantric meditations, such as the 'maṇḍalas' of ordinary body, speech and mind transforming into buddha body, speech and mind.

Mantra(s)

Sacred strings of tantric syllables, generally deriving from Sanskrit syllables considered sacred utterances in the ancient

Vedic traditions. Such strings of syllables are occasionally witnessed in early Buddhist texts, and applied to Buddhist purposes, and those called *dhāraṇī*s were important as blessings in Mahāyāna scriptures. In tantric Buddhism (also called the *Mantra Vehicle*), mantras became central in the meditative practices for the attainment of Enlightenment.

Māra
A personification of the forces of Ignorance and craving, a kind of Buddhist Devil who is said to have attempted to deflect the Buddha from his aspiration for Enlightenment.

Middle Way
The 'Middle Way' avoiding the extremes of indulgence in sense pleasures and of harsh asceticism, a central doctrine in early Buddhism. The term was extended also to include the avoidance of other 'extremes', such as clinging to existence or non-existence, eternity or annihilation, one or many. In Mahāyāna, an important philosophical school was called the 'Middle Way' (*Madhyamaka*).

Nirmāṇakāya
See: Triple Body of the Buddha (three *kāya*s).

Nirvāṇa/Nibbāna
See: Enlightenment.

Pāli Canon
The corpus of Buddhist scriptures preserved by the Theravāda school in Pāli, an Indian dialect related to Sanskrit.

Pāramitā(s)
The transcendent actions or perfections practised by a bodhisattva in order to attain the completely perfected Enlightenment of a buddha. The usual list has six components; there is also a commonly used list of ten.

Parinirvāṇa
The final Nirvāṇa: the passing away of a buddha or Arhat.

Paritta

'Protection': Pāli verses or discourses recited in Southern Buddhist practice to create protection or well-being.

Pratyekabuddha

One who becomes enlightened through their own efforts yet who does not systematically teach, a class of saints in early Buddhism.

Preta(s)

'Hungry ghosts': dissatisfied spirits who are said to experience intense suffering – a possible destiny after death.

Samādhi

Meditative absorption, the second of the Three Trainings in Buddhist practice.

Sambhogakāya

See: Triple Body of the Buddha (three *kāyas*).

Saṃsāra

The wheel or cycle of conditioned existence.

Samyak

Complete, perfect or whole. It is used to describe each aspect of the Eightfold Path, perfect or complete view, etc. It is also used in the phrase, *samyaksaṃbuddha, completely perfected Buddha.*

Sangha

The Buddhist community. The *Noble Sangha* are those who are irreversibly established on the path to Enlightenment, while the ordinary Sangha is the community of the Buddhist order. It usually specifically refers to the monastic community but can be extended to include lay practitioners.

Sarvāstivāda

An early Buddhist school that became prominent in Northern India. It left a lasting impact on Mahāyāna philosophy in that important Mahāyāna doctrines were developed in opposition to Sarvāstivāda positions.

Skandha/Khandha

The Aggregates: the five groups of the fundamental elements of worldly existence, the components of which make up an individual person – forms, feelings, perceptions/concepts, volitions/impulses, consciousness.

Śīla

Moral discipline, the first of the Three Trainings, and the second specific item in the list of the six bodhisattva transcendent actions.

Śramaṇa(s)

Groups of wandering ascetics or renouncers, common in the Buddha's time. Buddhism itself began as a *śramaṇa* movement.

Stūpa(s)

Constructions containing relics of the Buddha, which quickly became the focus of Buddhist pilgrimages and worship.

Sūtra/Sutta

The discourses attributed to the Buddha.

Tantra (and Tantric Buddhism)

At first not clearly distinguished from Mahāyāna sūtras, the tantras, like sūtras, were recognised as scriptures, appearing in the later period of Buddhism in India. Tantric Buddhism, known as the mantra vehicle (*mantrayāna*) or indestructible/thunderbolt vehicle (*vajrayāna*), grew up on the basis of these scriptures and their associated literature and practices. Related to a similar movement in Hinduism, the Buddhist tantras focus on techniques for transforming ordinary appearances, including the emotional afflictions, into enlightened wisdom manifestations, making use of visualisation, mantra recitation and ritual meditations.

Tathāgata

'Thus-Gone' or 'Thus-Come': this is a term which the Buddha used of himself, especially when emphasising his special status. It is also applied to later buddhas recognised in Mahāyāna Buddhism.

Theravāda
A Buddhist tradition deriving from one of the older schools in India, which was established and developed in Ceylon and became the dominant tradition in the Southern Buddhist countries (Sri Lanka, Thailand, Burma, Cambodia, Laos).

Triple Body of the Buddha (three *kāyas*)
Threefold 'body' in later Mahāyāna doctrine, consisting of the body of the Dharma or ultimate truth (*dharmakāya*), the perfected body of enjoyment (*sambhogakāya*), and the emanated body, the *nirmāṇakāya*.

Tripiṭaka/Tipiṭaka
The '3 baskets': a division of the Buddhist scriptures, comprising Vinaya, Sūtra and Abhidharma.

Tṛṣṇā
Craving, literally, 'thirst'.

Tuṣita heaven
A heavenly realm where the Buddha was supposed to reside in his penultimate life as a bodhisattva before taking his final birth in this world.

Vinaya
The section of Buddhist scriptures dealing with the monastic discipline.

BIBLIOGRAPHY

Aung San Suu Kyi 1995 *Freedom from Fear and Other Writings*, New York and London: Penguin Books.

Bechert, Heinz and Richard Gombrich (eds) 1984 *The World of Buddhism: Buddhist Monks and Nuns in Society and Culture*, London: Thames and Hudson.

Buddha Dharma Education Association and BuddhaNet *Buddhist Studies: for Primary and Secondary Students*. www.buddhanet.net/e-learning/buddhism/index.htm

Bullitt, John 2009 *Access to Insight: Readings in Theravada Buddhism*. English translations by various scholars. www.accesstoinsight.org/

Carrithers, Michael 1983 *The Buddha*, Oxford and New York: Oxford University Press.

Chah, Ajahn 1982 *Bodhinyāna*, Bung Wai Forest Monastery, Ubon Rajathani, Thailand.

Chikwang Sunim 1999 'A Strong Tradition Adapting to Change: The Nuns in Korea', in Thubten Chodron (ed.) *Blossoms of the Dharma: Living as a Buddhist Nun*, Berkeley: North Atlantic Books. www.koreanbuddhism.net/life/essay_view.asp?cat_seq=25&content_seq=487&priest_seq=0&page=1

Cleary, Thomas (Translated from Chinese) 1987 *The Flower Ornament Scripture. The Avatamsaka Sutra*. Boston and London: Shambhala (three volumes).

Conze, Edward 1959 *Buddhist Scriptures*, Harmondsworth: Penguin.

Conze, Edward 1973 *The Perfection of Wisdom in Eight Thousand Lines and its Verse Summary*, Delhi: Sri Satguru.

Corless, Roger 1989 *The Vision of Buddhism*, New York: Paragon.

Dalai Lama, The 1990 *Freedom in Exile: The Autobiography of The Dalai Lama*, New York: HarperCollins.

Darlington, Susan M. 2000 'Rethinking Buddhism and Development: The Emergence of Environmentalist Monks in Thailand'. *Journal of Buddhist Ethics* 7. www.buddhistethics.org/7/darlington001.html#one

Davidson, Ronald M. 1995 'The Litany of Names of Mañjuśrī', in Donald S. Lopez (ed.) *Religions of India in Practice*, Princeton: Princeton University Press, pp. 104–25.

Feuchtwang, Stephan 2001 *Popular Religion in China*. London and New York: RoutledgeCurzon.

Gethin, Rupert 1998 *The Foundations of Buddhism*, Oxford: Oxford University Press.

Goldstein, Melvyn C. and Matthew Kapstein 1998 *Buddhism in Contemporary Tibet: Religious Revival and Cultural Identity*, Berkeley: University of California Press.

Gombrich, Richard 1990 'How the Mahāyāna Began', in T. Skorupski (ed.) *The Buddhist Forum Volume I*, London: SOAS, University of London, pp. 21–30.

Gombrich, Richard 2006 *Theravāda Buddhism*, Abingdon and New York: Routledge.

Gombrich, Richard and Gananath Obeyesekere 1988 *Buddhism Transformed: Religious Change in Sri Lanka*, Princeton: Princeton University Press.

Gyatso, Janet 2006 'A Partial Genealogy of the Lifestory of Ye shes mtsho rgyal'. *Journal of the International Association of Tibetan Studies*, no. 2: 1–27. www.thdl.org?id=T2719

Harvey, Peter 1990 *An Introduction to Buddhism: Teachings, History and Practices*, Cambridge: Cambridge University Press.

Harvey, Peter 2000 *An Introduction to Buddhist Ethics: Foundations, Values and Issues*, Cambridge: Cambridge University Press.

Hodge, S. (trans.) 2003 *The Mahā-Vairocana-Abhisaṃbodhi Tantra with Buddhaguhya's Commentary*, London: RoutledgeCurzon.

Jacoby, Sarah In press '"This Inferior Female Body:" Reflections on Life as a Treasure Revealer through the Autobiographical Eyes of Se ra mKha' 'gro (bde ba'i rdo rje, 1892–1940)', in *Proceedings of the International Association for Tibetan Studies* 11, Halle, International Institute for Tibetan and Buddhist Studies.

Kawanami, Hiroko 2007 'The Bhikkhunī Ordination Debate: Global Aspirations, Local Concerns, with Special Emphasis on the Views of the Monastic Community in Burma'. *Buddhist Studies Review*, 24 no. 2: 226–44.

Kee Nanayon, Upasika 2003 'Pure and Simple', Thanissaro Bhikkhu (trans), Khao Suan Luang Dhamma Community. www.dharmaweb.org/index.php/Pure_&_Simple_by_Upasika_Kee_Nanayon

Khyentse Rinpoche, Dilgo 2006 *Zurchungpa's Testament*, Padmakara Translation Group, Snow Lion.

Lamotte, Étienne 1976 *The Teaching of Vimalakīrti (Vimalakīrtinirdeśa)*. Translated by S. Boin. Pali Text Society, London, distributed by Routledge and Kegan Paul.

Lopez, Donald (ed.) 1995 *Buddhism in Practice*, Princeton: Princeton University Press.

Mahidol University 2002 *An Illustrated Life of the Buddha*, Bangkok. www.budsir.org/MenuEng.htm

Muhlberger, Steve 1998 'Democracy in Ancient India'. www.nipissingu.ca/department/history/muhlberger/histdem/indiadem.htm#text52

Nārada Mahā Thera 1973 *The Buddha and His Teachings*, Colombo: Vajirārāma.

Patrul Rinpoche 1994 *The Words of My Perfect Teacher*. Padmakāra Translation Committee, San Francisco: Harper Collins.

Pratyutpanna Samādhi Sūtra, The, translated by Lokakṣema, and translated from the Chinese by Paul Harrison, 1998, in *BDK English Tripiṭaka* 25-II, 25-III, Berkeley: Bukkyō Dendō Kyōkai, pp. 1–116.

Pruitt, William (trans.) 1998 *Commentary on Verses of Therīs*, Oxford: Pali Text Society.

Pye, Michael 1979 *The Buddha*, London: Duckworth.

Reader, Ian 1991 *Religion in Contemporary Japan*, London: Macmillan.

Rewata Dhamma, U and Bhikkhu Bodhi 'Introduction' to *A Comprehensive Manual of Abhidhamma: The Abhidhammattha Sangaha* of Acariya Anuruddha, Bhikkhu Bodhi (general editor), Mahathera Narada (editor and translator of Pali Text). 1993 Buddhist Publication Society, Kandy, Sri Lanka; *Access to Insight* edition 1995. www.accesstoinsight.org/lib/authors/bodhi/abhiman.html

Ricard, Matthieu 1994 *The Life of Shabkar. The Autobiography of a Tibetan Yogin*. New York: The State University of New York Press (SUNY).

The *Saddharmapuṇḍarīka (Lotus Sūtra)*, translated by H. Kern, 1884, *Sacred Books of the East*, Vol XXI. www.sacred-texts.com/bud/lotus/index.htm

Samuel, Geoffrey 1993 *Civilized Shamans: Buddhism in Tibetan Societies*, Washington and London: Smithsonian Institution Press.

Schopen, Gregory 1997 *Bones, Stones, and Buddhist Monks*, Honolulu, University of Hawai'i Press.

Schwartz, Ronald 1994 'Buddhism, Nationalist Protest and the State in Tibet', in P. Kvaerne (ed.) *Tibetan Studies*, Oslo: Institute for Comparative Research in Human Culture, pp. 728–38.

Snellgrove, David L 1987 *Indo-Tibetan Buddhism: Indian Buddhists and their Tibetan successors*, London: Serindia.

Strong, John 2001 *The Buddha, A Short Biography*, Oxford: Oneworld.

Tambiah, Stanley 1976 *World Conqueror and World Renouncer: A Study of Buddhism and Polity in Thailand against a Historical Background*, Cambridge and New York: Cambridge University Press.

Tambiah, Stanley 1984 *The Buddhist Saints of the Forest and the Cult of Amulets: A Study in Charisma, Hagiography, Sectarianism and Millennial Buddhism*, Cambridge: Cambridge University Press.

Tedesco, Frank M. 1996 'Rites for the Unborn Dead: Abortion and Buddhism in Contemporary Korea'. www.buddhapia.com/eng/tedesco/kjabo.html, reproduced from *Korea Journal*, 36 no. 2: 61–74.

Thich Nhat Hanh 1999 *Interbeing: Fourteen Guidelines for Engaged Buddhism*, Berkeley: Parallax Press.

The Tipitaka www.metta.lk/tipitaka/

Tsomo, Karma Lekshe (ed.) *Sakyadhīta: Daughters of the Buddha*, Ithaca: Snow Lion Publications.

Walshe, Maurice 1995 *The Long Discourses of the Buddha: A Translation of the Dīgha Nikāya*, Boston: Wisdom Publications.

Warder, A.K. *Indian Buddhism*, Delhi: Motilal Banarsidass.

Wijayaratna, Mohan 1990 *Buddhist Monastic Life: According to the Texts of the Theravāda Tradition*, Cambridge: Cambridge University Press.

Williams, Liz 2000 'A Whisper in the Silence: Nuns before Mahāpajāpatī?' *Buddhist Studies Review*, 17 no. 2: 167–73.

Williams, Liz 2002 'Red Rust, Robbers and Rice Fields: Women's Part in the Precipitation of the Decline of the Dhamma' *Buddhist Studies Review*, 19 no. 1: 41–47.

Williams, Paul 2008 *Mahāyāna Buddhism. The Doctrinal Foundations*, Abingdon: Taylor and Francis.

Williams, Paul and Anthony Tribe 2000 *Buddhist Thought: A Complete Introduction to the Indian Tradition*, London and New York: Routledge.

Wittgenstein, Ludwig 1979 'Remarks on Frazer's *Golden Bough*', edited by Rush Rhees, translated by A.C. Miles, revised by Rush Rhees. Retford: Brynmill Press.

Woodhead, Linda, Paul Fletcher, Hiroko Kawanami and David Smith (eds) 2009 *Religions in the Modern World*, Routledge.

INDEX